What people are saying about *Lea*

"This book does an excellent job of demonstrating why it's important for organizations to foster collaboration and leadership at all levels and in every person. It offers concrete steps all members can take to create a truly collaborative environment. Very insightful and useful!"
Jani Jackson, MEd, Founder, Develop Your Team

"To become a great leader is to be well practiced in leadership. This is a manual to help all of us practice those skills, regardless of where we are in our careers. As an experiential educator who has worked extensively with adult and corporate clients, this book resonated with me. It will spark reflection for a leader at any level of an organization."
Paul J. Hutchinson, MS, PhD, Boston University Questrom School of Business

"Greg has effectively broken down one of the most common business buzzwords—'collaboration'—into actionable and practical concepts. His novel perspective on helping each other ask better questions is a powerful core piece of collaboration."
Chad Littlefield, CEO, We!™

"Greg Robinson has clearly defined the role of a leader and redefined the nebulous concept of team work. He calls it collaboration. He defines it, shines a light on the path so we can find it, then presents the issues that might prevent us from getting there. This is a must read for the leader who is serious about creating a work culture that people want to be part of, while keeping focused on results."
John Rogers, Team and Leadership Center Director, Montreat College

"*Leading From Where You Are* will open your eyes to what true collaboration looks like and how to create an environment where people are selflessly willing to share ideas and resources for the good of the whole."
Sam Sikes, author of *A Foundation of Trust*

"The action-learning process taught me to truly open my eyes, ears and mind. It changed my view of teams. Now, I see that every personality can fit into and enjoy the team situation when using respect, trust and honesty as a basis for working together. As a project manager, I have more tools for solving people issues, fewer limiting assumptions, and practical techniques for turning differences into resources. This process supports a mature and grown-up way of doing business."
Kieran Major, Principal Program Manager at American Airlines

Other books by Greg Robinson...

Teams for a New Generation: An Introduction to Collective Learning

Teams for a New Generation: A Facilitator's Field Guide
with Mark Rose

A Leadership Paradox: Influencing Others by Defining Yourself
with Mark Rose

Adventure and the Way of Jesus:
An Experiential Approach to Spiritual Formation

Lessons of the Way: Using Adventure Activities to Explore the Way of Jesus
with Mark Rose

Greg Robinson

LEADING
FROM
WHERE
YOU ARE

How Every Person Can Help or Hinder the Collaborative Culture

Wood N Barnes Publishing
2309 N. Willow, Suite A, Bethany, OK
800.678.0621

This publication is sold with the understanding that the publisher is not engaged in rendering psychological, medical, or other professional services.

Interior design by Ramona Cunningham

Printed in the United States of America
ISBN 978-1-939019-21-9

To my Dad who taught me patience, humility and the
work ethic underlying my understanding of leadership.

Content

Introduction   ix

Chapter One: Collaboration: The 21ˢᵗ Century Requirement   1
Collaboration Defined   2
Collaboration as a Quality of Interaction   5
Collaboration as an Orientation Toward Work   7
Creating a Place That Works for All   13

Chapter Two: Your Workplace and Emotional Process   16
Emotional Process   18
Unconscious Development   21

Chapter Three: Self-Definition as a Leadership Practice   29
Strategies for Self-Definition   32
Sustaining Self-Defined Perspective   36
Tactics of Self-Defined Leaders   39
    Presence   39
    Distance   42
    Direction   43

Chapter Four: Looking Outward: Moving From
Self-Awareness to Other-Awareness   46
Meeting Reviews   47
    Difference   47
    Decisions   48
    Emotion   49
    Responsibility   50
    Trust   50
    Openness   51
Alternative Ways of Building Other-Awareness

Chapter Five: Developing the System: How to Help
Others Become Self-Defined   53
Building the Container   53
The Practice of Action-Learning   54

Perception   67
Presence   68
    Forces in Tension   68
    Sabotage   73

Chapter Six: Triangles and the False Hope of Gossip   77
  Conflict Strategies   78
    Linear Strategies   78
    Triangles   78
  A Systems Approach to Conflict   80
    Tolerance of Tension   81
  Illusions of Trust   82

Conslusion   83

Acknowledgements   85

Appendices   86

Resources   91

About the Author   95

Introduction

There are days when I get up and can't wait to get to work. The challenge of the day is exhilarating and the potential for a satisfying accomplishment is within reach. This was not one of those days. I had been asked to consult with a cross-functional team that was trying to design a new strategy for college relations for a Fortune 500 company. The group was made up of business unit representatives from three distinct divisions, which were all at different points in their development. This group's task was to develop a collaborative and creative solution to better the company.

I knew going in this would be no simple task. There were too many contributing factors. There was an extremely aggressive time frame, there were competing powers in the form of two directors (who obviously did not trust one another), there was a history with this team, and there were the organizational culture factors. The cultural factors that seemed to play a considerable role included the resistance of all business unit groups to work in collaboration with each other, a sense that Corporate was trying to take power over the business units and control them, an ingrained niceness that prevented open confrontation and encouraged passive-aggressive methods, the perpetual resistance of the company to work with anyone, and the residual of a command and control hierarchy that was transitioning out. This was just one of many cross-functional attempts I had taken part in for a company that historically was a holding company but now was attempting to transition to an enterprise. The rhetoric was there but the will was often lacking.

I had observed this group over six days and thirty-seven hours of meetings. They continually moved off point, chasing minute details. There was a good bit of passive-aggressive behavior and there was virtually no creative thinking. At more than one point, each of the leaders came to me and said, "You are going to have to make us do this." Even the leaders lacked vision and facilitative capability to bring the group into a shared vision. It was interesting that the team seemed to know how difficult they were making this, openly commenting and joking about it in our sessions. They did not seem able to learn from experience. Even a direct confrontation on my part concerning their defense mechanism elicited little conversation and no change of behavior. Insight did not influence them. This was a strange phenomenon since the individual members of the team were very competent.

This story would not be so distressing, were it not for the fact that it happens thousands of times a day in thousands of organizations of all types, all over the world. There is a need and often a stated desire to collaborate (i.e., to tap into the collective intelligence the team and discover new and effective ways to work). But the ability to actually do it is severely lacking. There is a quote that has been one of my favorites over the years:

> If the world is going to change, it will not be by old minds with new programs but by new minds with no programs at all (Quinn, 1999, p. 7).

If we are to develop and sustain a collaborative way of working, we must find new ways of understanding. We cannot continue to chase techniques hoping to harness our unwilling hearts to be collaborative. We must see this endeavor in a very different way.

I am going to attempt the impossible. I want to suggest that rather than something to be avoided or endured, meetings are the life blood of human organizations. It is in our intentional conversations (meetings) that we either reinforce our old divided mindsets or we discover and practice something new. Now I know this might be an uphill climb but I believe that the problem with meetings is not that they exist; it is that we do not know how to do them. Meetings are where the collective creates more than the individual ever could. It is the place where culture is created and sustained through public reflection. It is where decisions are made and problems are solved, and it is

The problem with meetings is not that they exist; it is that we do not know how to do them.

where we can get better at doing both if we will practice with effort and integrity. So whether you are a leader in a corporation or not-for-profit, a faculty member or administrator in a college or university, a facilitator or trainer working to help groups improve, a member of a family business or even a parent, how you interact with others determines the quality of choices that are made and the tone of making future decisions. One more thing—whether you have a formal position of leadership or not, every day you interact with others, you are a source of influence. You exercise leadership. The only question is, "Will your influence be positive and empowering or divisive and fragmenting?" This is a book for leaders as long as you are willing to confirm that we are all leaders at some level, every day, in every system of which we are a part.

> We are all leaders at some level, every day, in every system of which we are a part.
>
> "Will your influence be positive and empowering or divisive and fragmenting?"

This is not a quick fix guide for leaders to suppress bad habits and cover up ill will. It is not a collection of gimmicks and tricks to mask symptoms of poor interaction. Rather this is an effort to look at the root causes of our inept efforts to talk and listen to one another. It is a description of pot holes and quagmires that distract from meaningful interaction. It is a discussion of how we can improve our organizations by freeing ourselves from the anxiety and fears that keep our best thinking captive.

Though I use meetings as a common context for looking at how human dynamics often work out, we must realize that a process is only as capable as the people who are involved. So, a good amount of time will be spent looking into how we talk and listen, advocate and inquire, influence and are influenced by others—all of which can be thought of in the context of leadership.

The core of the ideas we will explore come from my twenty-five years as a facilitator, professor, manager, and business owner—from both the helping side for others and the doing side as a member of organizational meetings. Most of my adult life, I have been pursuing ways to create sustainable change that leads to long-term health and

growth. I have done so in the context of corporations, small businesses, universities, and even religious institutions. We need to be better at
thinking together because the complexity
of our world requires all of us to contribute. The kind of change I am searching
for does not come with the acquisition
of information or certain answers, it only
comes by asking questions. It is a result
of watching what others have tried—out of inspiration or desperate
necessity—and found to work for them. We watch not to mimic but
to discover the questions that were asked to come upon the new idea
and to let the application of a different way of thinking spur us to
think about our own contexts differently than we have. To do this we
need a great deal of emotional maturity and critical thinking, which is
exactly what we are going to explore in this book.

> We need to be better at thinking together because the complexity of our world requires all of us to contribute.

One of the "new frames" I want readers to consider is that a good
leader does not need a formal position, title, or authority. Every single
one of us has the ability to influence our place of work because we are
a member of a system. Each of us, should we have the courage to step
out, can "lead from where we are." We just need to understand how
the systems work so we can understand how to participate in them to
promote the greatest possible health of the system. So this book is focused on helping us understand human systems and how purposeful,
intentional members who are not afraid to have their own thoughts
and make room for different perspectives can create a culture of collaboration.

For nearly 20 years, authors have been making the case that organizations are better off when they have leaders at all levels of the
organization.

> At any given point in time, I believe, this is the best predictor of
> whether or not a company will win in the near and long term.
> Technologies, products and even demographic shifts come and
> go. But a company that continually produces leaders at all levels
> is here to stay ... (Tichey, Noel & Cohen, 1997, p. 6).

If this is true, then how can there be enough positions to have enough leaders to respond to the pace of work today? And if you could create enough positions for leadership to be a position, would you have enough people left to follow? No, in a world where everyone must make decisions that could impact the organization's brand, reputation, work processes and culture, leadership is not about position, title and authority. Leadership is about influence and influence is a combination of awareness and engagement. True leaders allow the "leadership influence" to move around a team or organization based on who has the best awareness of the issue at hand and who can articulate and integrate ideas well enough to bring people along. Leadership is a result of who is continuing to learn and change and who is willing to step out first and demonstrate a different way for others. In this case, leadership can exist in any person, at any time, at any level of the organization. The intern who asks a naïve but timely question, the tested veteran who asks for help, the CEO who dares to listen to voices not generally considered—all are examples of how awareness and engagement can begin to shift the culture to genuinely resemble a collaborative enterprise.

> Leadership is about influence and influence is a combination of awareness and engagement.

The Structure of the Book

My goal is to provide a very practical book that anyone can read, a guide to making meaningful choices for themselves that can lead to sustainable and effective impact on their organizations. So we begin in chapter one by understanding what collaboration is and why it is so important. Not every situation requires collaboration but when it is needed it is essential. Collaboration is not something that can be developed well on the fly or in moments of crisis. It is a capacity that must be built so it is present when needed.

> Collaboration cannot be developed well on the fly or in moments of crisis. It is a capacity that must be built so it is present when needed.

Chapter two looks at the work place as an emotional system. Collaboration is a systemic process that is amplified or dissipated by the level of courage and anxiety present in the system. The path toward a culture of collaboration is through the personal responsibility of each member; therefore, how to best participate and influence the team or organization requires that we understand how human systems function. With an understanding of the system, we are then free to explore the kind of individuals who can influence a team or organization in order to reduce anxiety and promote greater health.

Chapter three defines the process whereby leaders become self-differentiated. The result of increasing our level of self-definition is that we can help calm the anxious system and thus release the capabilities that have been held captive by fear and uncertainty. I make a bold statement in this chapter. Many leadership theories of the last 100 years have focused the leader's attention to those he or she leads. Traits, skills, styles, transactions, and visions are all designed to get others to do something the leader desires. But true leadership—leadership that builds the capacity of a team or organization to be resilient, sustainable, responsive, and effective—places its focus elsewhere. This kind of leader starts with the self. Defining oneself, developing deep levels of self-awareness, being able to manage boundaries because of that self-awareness, and remaining intentional rather than reactive is the destination for the self-differentiated leader. It is not enough, however, that a leader is self-defined, he or she must make room for and pursue the same kind of self-differentiated growth and maturity in all members of the team or organization. For a self-differentiated leader understands that the only way to move beyond the petty, recurring problems that constrain true collaboration is to help develop mature companions in the organization.

Chapter four looks to help those who would increase their level of self-differentiation understand how to move from self-awareness to other-awareness. The ability to see this awareness in the interactions of others allows us the possibility to help, to step in from a different perspective and thus influence a more healthy place, which is not determined by the unattended anxiety in the room.

Chapter five takes a look at the forces within systems that work against self-differentiation and collaboration. We explore how to promote a context, a container, if you will, that enhances the ability to be collaborative and, at the same time, develops a level of maturity and self-definition. Secrecy, gossip, politeness are all temptations that offer the power of being "special" but only bring division, immaturity, and resentment. The self-differentiated leader must understand how to combat these forces and how not to unwittingly collude with them. Practices that promote collaboration and form the collaborative mind-set in us are included here. It is pointless to have a good model of leadership if we do not have practical and useful ways of putting our leadership into action. Collaborative problem-solving grows out of the action-learning process—a simple, disciplined way of interacting that is incredibly flexible. It is simple enough to be used for quick, well understood issues and robust enough to handle really complex issues. It is the one process I have found that promotes both personal responsibility and collaboration at the same time. It is a terrific place to practice being the kind of mature leader so many organizations are lacking today.

> Collaborative problem-solving grows out of the action-learning process—a simple, disciplined way of interacting that is incredibly flexible.

I will end with a warning. If you want quick fixes, stop reading now. If you are not yet fed up with more of the same, more of trying to motivate the unmotivated, of trying to fix others, of trying to control teams of limited maturity and capacity, then this book is not for you. On the other hand, if you want to do more than put band aids on a cancer, you might discover the way less travelled here. And as Robert Frost tells us, "... it has made all the difference" (Frost, 1916).

In Case You Are Interested...

The primary goal of this book is to provide clear and actionable strategies for everyone in an organization to grow their self-awareness and emotional stamina in order to create an openness to influence that collaboration requires. It is beyond our intent to provide an exhaustive review of the research. Our desire is to make the foundational ideas upon which this perspective is built accessible to the widest number of people possible.

However, we also know that many readers will be curious about the research which has led to a growing body of literature pointing us in the direction of this book. So we have added the sections, In Case You Are Interested..., to provide some bread crumbs of the literature to encourage your own exploration of the underlying research.

CHAPTER ONE

Collaboration: The 21ˢᵗ Century Requirement

"One of the biggest steps an organization takes is when
its people develop as much commitment to collective success
as they do to individual success."

For decades now, organizations have been seeking ways to capitalize on the creativity and intelligence of their members. Though there has been a great deal of effort, it is still a mystery to unravel. Here are some facts from a corporate setting that paint the picture. The ability to maintain consistent collaboration has remained elusive though it is widely sought. In a 2007 Center for Creative Leadership study, 91% of respondents agreed, "Teams are central to organization success." Additionally, 87% of respondents said, "Collaborating with other teams is essential for success." In 2011, Ernst and Chrobot-Mason (2011) echoed similar sentiments when 86% of the executives in their survey expressed the significant importance of collaborating across boundaries but only 7% thought they were very good at such collaboration. In a 2016 Deloitte report, only 21% of respondents believed they had expertise in building cross-functional teams. The sobering fact, as outlined in the study, was that only about half of the organizations surveyed thought their teams met the company's expectations. For most organizations, teams have been fully integrated and internal team interactions can be effective; however, working across boundaries is less successful. In a 2005 McKinsey study, 80% of executives agreed "effective coordination across product, functional, and geographical lines was crucial for growth," yet only 25% of those same executives said they were effective at working across boundaries. As the research indicates, we have been chasing answers to creating real collaboration for over a decade and we are still missing the mark to a great extent.

The speed, complexity, and volume of work today requires an integrated organization capable of collaborating consistently at all levels and across all parts of the organization. Even leadership is being reframed into a collective process requiring multiple, diverse perspectives to be brought together to identify sustainable solutions and effective enterprise strategies (Martin, 2005).

So, if collaboration is so important, why are we not very good at it? More importantly, why are we not improving substantially even though time and resources have been concentrated on this area? It could be that the answer to these questions boils down to

1) a lack of understanding true collaboration,
2) a lack of discipline and commitment to processes that are truly collaborative,
3) a lack of maturity and self-awareness required to really collaborate, and finally
4) not using collaboration in the right way.

Collaboration Defined

A number of words are often used interchangeably, with people assuming they all have the same meaning. Teamwork, cooperation, collaboration, synergy are common words in organizational vocabulary. There is, in my opinion, a qualitative difference between the ability to work together without conflict while sharing information or resources and the ability to truly collaborate. If we are to gain expertise rather than maintain the image of collaboration without the substance, we need to clarify the definition of collaboration.

Let's start by comparing cooperation and collaboration. Cooperation is a state whereby members of a team or organization share information, resources, and people. It is, however, a state whereby members maintain their autonomy and tolerate differences for a period of time before returning to their rightful places. It is not that cooperation is bad, it is that it does not go far enough. Collaboration, by contrast, is a form of relationship marked by trust where "there is mutuality of influence and learning that enables each person to grow (learn) beyond what would have been possible for either individual alone" (George Mason University). In collaborative interactions there is an openness which leads to all persons being different after their encounter. It is not a temporary state of tolerance. Fundamentally, collaboration is a struggle between the need for autonomy and control versus deep levels of trust.

> Collaborative interactions create an openness which leads to all persons being different after their encounter.

In my practice, I have noticed some common steps from autonomy to collaboration which have been consistent across many teams and organizations.

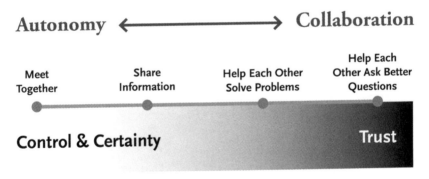

Figure 1.1: Autonomy ⟵⟶ Collaboration Time-Line

Meet Together

The first steps for many teams is just to meet together. I have worked with hundreds of teams over the years, and it still amazes me how many teams do not make time to meet together. Somehow there is a belief that teams can be healthy even though they do not have mean-

There must be regular, meaningful, and intentional interaction between the people with whom you want to collaborate.

ingful interaction. I know this is true because many seemed surprised that meeting together was such an important issue. But if collaboration is to have any hope of being developed, there must be regular, meaningful, and intentional interaction between the people with whom you want to collaborate.

● Share Information

Once people experience some meetings that are useful and mostly successful, they will often take the next step along the path and start to share information. This is the basis of most staff meetings in most organizations. People begin to open up and are willing to talk about what they are doing and pass along information they have come across. Though this is a step in the right direction it is a long way from collaboration. The problem is many teams and organizations are satisfied when they reach this point. The problem is that we are still far down the control and certainty end. Who determines what information gets shared? The person doing the sharing. What do we tend to be willing to share with co-workers and supervisors? Those things that are going well or we believe we have figured out. There is some sense of sharing in this type of engagement but there is very little vulnerability and openness to being influenced by others.

● Help Each Other Solve Problems

The next step of progression is often the initial extension of real trust and that is when people start asking others to help them solve their problems. Now this is an expo-

Often, what we think is the problem is only a symptom of the problem.

Unless we are willing to question our understanding of our problem, we may find we are solving the wrong problem.

nential step beyond just sharing information, but it is not yet fully on the collaborative end of the continuum. The reason for this is twofold. First, even if a person is willing to ask for help and share a problem, it is that person who determines what problems will be revealed. Second, the definition of the problem presented is assumed to be right. No one really questions the definition of the stated problem, but simply begins to start solving what is presented. Often though, what we think is the problem is only a symptom of the problem. We often see only parts of an issue and unless we are willing to question our understanding of our own problem, we may find we are solving the wrong problem.

● Help Each Other Ask Better Questions

This brings us to the most collaborative action on the continuum. When we begin to really extend trust, to allow the perspectives of others to influence us, then we not only ask for help with problems but we allow others to question our very understanding of the problem. We are open to probing questions that might challenge our assumptions about the issue. As a result, we accept the possibility that we might have to reframe our issue or redefine it altogether. The result is that we become clearer about what is most important for us to solve and we tend to more often solve the right things. In short, collaboration could be understood as the willingness to come into contact with new questions.

Collaboration as a Quality of Interaction

The time-line shown in Figure 1.1 (page 3) helps us hone in on a definition of collaboration. Collaboration could be understood as the willingness to encounter new questions. The only way to really encounter new and challenging questions is to have a certain quality of interaction with others.

Not too long ago, a colleague come into my office, and we started chatting. I'd worked around him for two years, and other than his name and what he teaches, I didn't really know much more about him. So, I decided to take this opportunity to deepen the conversation with him. I asked some questions about his field of study and some things I had read lately. I opened with questions. Looking back, the conversation did not go badly but for me it was an insight into collaborative interactions. We talked for several minutes. He shared his thoughts on the author and book that I had asked about. I was gathering information and he was giving it. The problem is, it didn't go any further. For those with whom I really collaborate, there would be a give and take of perspectives. He would ask my thoughts, and I would continue to explore his. Over time, we could discover something together that we could not discover alone. But what we did was spend a pleasant few minutes and off he went. I suspect he was comfortable in the role of expert, in which my questions seemed to put him. All too often we settle for this. We do not seem to be naturally inclined to be collaborative, to participate in learning collectively. We tend to pass information around and go about our business.

So how will we know if the quality of our interaction is collaborative or not? The following are three suggestions:

First, we know we are collaborating when we are surfacing our assumptions and challenging them. **Collaboration is not just changing what we think but how we think.** When we ask questions and let others question us, we can begin to gain some clarity about the assumptions we hold and why we hold them. Now, having assumptions is not necessarily bad; however, not knowing that I hold assumptions can be

> When we question and allow questions, we begin to gain some clarity about the assumptions we hold and why we hold them.

damaging. The first purpose of collaborative interaction is to surface our individual and collective assumptions and test them for accuracy. We may not change our assumptions but if we choose to keep them we will also be able to change them when necessary.

Second, we know we are collaborating when **we become more intentional and less reactive to others.** One of the biggest hurdles to collaboration is that we fear differences. When we encounter something that is different than what we know or think, we are often fearful. When fear sets in, we often dismiss an idea or person without really thinking. We react emotionally to a perceived threat and we do what is necessary to return to a state of security. Collaboration requires

emotional risk. It requires us to be uncomfortable, and it requires us to encounter ideas that
are different from our own. Consequently, we

> Collaboration requires
> emotional risk.

need to be purposeful in the face of stress and we need to value differences as a stimulant to true learning.

Finally, when we are challenging our assumptions and remain intentional in valuing difference, we can achieve the third characteristic
of collaborative interaction. **We begin to gain a broader perspective.**
With emotional reactivity out of the way, we can begin to entertain
a variety of perspectives on an issue. We may not agree with them all
but if we at least hear them and respect them, we will be more knowl-
edgeable than we would be without them.

Collaboration as an Orientation Toward Work

There is another way of thinking about collaboration that moves
beyond the interactions between or among people. It is a perspective
that focuses on the larger culture, promoting a particular kind of leadership philosophy. Collaboration
as an orientation toward work is
a way of thinking about one's individual role, resources, and influence as being in the midst of
something bigger. It is a philoso-

> Collaboration as an orientation toward
> work is a way of thinking about one's
> individual role, resources, and influence
> as being in the midst of something bigger.

phy that promotes commitment to both the local (department, team,
business unit) and the global (the enterprise, cross-business unit, perhaps even the industry). This grander collaborative perspective sets the
tone for a culture of shared interest, shared vision, and the pursuit of
shared success by all relevant members. It is a leadership perspective
that does not minimize the whole by maximizing parts. It is the underlying mental model that will actually invest and sustain the more
localized practice of collaboration as a quality of interaction. So what
is this elusive culture? It is built on the following values and principles.

All invested parties enjoy stature and influence in decision-making.

If collaboration is a process of mutual influence and shared learning, it makes sense that the involved parties have the right to speak their mind and present a perspective that has impact on the decisions being made. Many times, organizational change language speaks of teams and collaborative effort, when in reality all the decisions about the change were made in an office somewhere by just a few people "in the know." Once the decisions are rolled out, although town hall meetings make space for questions, there is no real time or permission given to dissent. So, if we want a truly collaborative culture, we must promote practices that call for and value real input from multiple perspectives in decision-making. It is true this will take more time on the front end of decisions, but an enormous amount of time is made up on the back end implementation of decisions. Decisions made in a collaborative way often lack the resistance and sabotage that accompanies change that is done to others.

> A truly collaborative culture promotes practices that call for and value real input from multiple perspectives in decision-making.

There is a word of warning or a potential pitfall we must avoid here. Decision-making that is inclusive and participatory can become prisoner of the immature and resistant if we are not careful. This value of inclusiveness does not say that every person has a stake in every decision that is made. That sort of practice is marred in a lack of trust and will lead to quagmires and inaction. I once observed the quarterly business meeting of a division of a large company. My role was to assess what was happening in the meeting and make recommendations to improve it. One of the things I noticed was that the group was held captive to its unspoken value of ownership and responsibility. Every leader in the group thought they should have a veto or final approval on decisions that were made but no one wanted to take responsibility for the actions. Though the reputation of this company was one of being nice, professional, and polite, it was limited by a deep sense of mistrust. Leaders who had, at best, a peripheral interest on decisions, would hijack conversations resulting in a decision-making process so painful that no decisions were ever made.

For a collaborative culture to thrive, there is a basic level of trust that must be ingrained. There must be trust that those who have a real stake in decisions will be involved and will have presence, a voice, and a platform to be heard and understood.

Let me give you an example of how this can work. One of my roles is program manager for an outdoor center for leadership development. It is a working camp that acts as a leadership training lab for undergraduate and graduate students. This past summer, two of the undergraduate students on staff broke a policy after they had been warned about their behavior. Moreover, when they broke the policy again, it was at the house of a constituent of the camp with long ties and family history. In other words, they broke the policy in public. It was determined after a series of conversations between myself, the director of support services (he runs all investigations into serious infractions), and the site manager (a long-time contact of the camp supporter who reported the behavior) that the young men should be sent home. I then spoke to the program manager who was the supervisor responsible for the two offenders. She listened to what we said and seemed to accept our decision. After a night's sleep and thinking more about the decision, she asked us to consider other options. She made a case for a lesser response. We talked through options and arrangements until we came to one that worked for all, including the young men whose fate we held. In the end, the offenders were reassigned to the direct supervision of the program manager; they lost their roles on staff but remained close to their programs in a support role. They were given the opportunity to redeem themselves by how they acted from then on, the level of responsibility they took for their actions, and demonstrating they could hear the guidance of their leaders. It worked out well. In many organizations, this decision would not have been discussed, explored, and questioned. It would have been handed down. In our situation, because the leaders involved were willing to hear all the parties and recognized the wisdom in the program manager's alternative perspective, a much better solution was achieved.

All parties commit to transparency of motives and intents.

One of the requirements of collaborative cultures is a commitment to no surprises. Things change, sometimes information is wrong and decisions don't work out. These can be survived as learning experiences. But what will deeply damage the collaborative culture is when people hold back information, motives, agendas which then lead to a less than honest conversation. This, in my experience, is a more prominent problem than most people realize. Most teams, which also means that most decisions, in organizations today are cross-functional. This also means that every team member has multiple agendas which guide their perspective and actions and determine their loyalties. There are the desires of their individual leaders and departments that want a certain outcome. There is the team with which they are serving that has as its goal to be successful. There is also personal ambition and perhaps ethics that demand attention. The real danger here is that most of these motives and intents are not spoken of and perhaps are not even in the awareness of the participants.

> A lack of openness about existing information, motives, and agendas can deeply damage the collaborative culture.

Again, collaboration requires trust, and trust requires transparency. It is not people holding onto these differing values, desires, or perspectives that erodes collaboration, it is the lack of openness to their existence. Collaborative leaders are committed to valuing differences and finding solutions that work for all. This does not mean that everyone gets their way, but it does mean that all agendas are put on the table and are considered as part of the equation. Trust is built in an atmosphere where there are no surprises.

> Trust is built in an atmosphere where there are no surprises.

Actions reflect a commitment to excellence and shared purpose.

One of the biggest steps an organization takes is when its people develop as much commitment to collective success as they do to individual success. This mindset is a prerequisite to all the other components of a collaborative mindset. Without the larger goal of collective success, leaders and members will not likely share resources, promote transparency, or create solutions and agreements that are good for the whole of the organization. This requires individuals to first see the big picture and how the system works as a whole. Many times decisions are made with too narrow a scope. When individuals understand not only what their job is in their department and how that job fits into larger processes, but also how their department fits into the larger business model of the company, there is the perspective to make choices that could be less successful to the individual in the short run but more sustainable for the whole in the long run. This also requires individuals to have a longer time horizon. A focus on the urgency of short-term goals or solutions limits our ability to understand how a less comfortable choice now will create better options for everyone later. This expansive perspective enables agility and flexibility of the organization because it enables the next shared principle.

> One of the biggest steps an organization takes is when its people develop as much commitment to collective success as they do to individual success.

All parties commit to bring their best resources to the project.

This is the testing ground of a real collaborative culture. Are leaders willing to share their resources with other departments just because that is the best use of those resources? Often meetings go nowhere and projects fall apart because departments are not willing to share resources with other departments. In fact, there is a game within the game where departments try to get the best people, the biggest budgets and the most influence because it is assumed these things will bring security. Yet, this mindset is short-sighted and limiting. What brings long-term security is the survival of the whole and the ability of the organization to adjust and adapt quickly. Mature leaders recognize that the organization should put its resources in those places where they are most needed. They trust that in the long run being helpful is more valuable than being in charge.

All parties commit to conceptualize, negotiate, and implement mutually beneficial outcomes.

We started this chapter with the idea that collaboration is really a process of deep trust. We do not trust for the sake of trusting but to enable something else. That something else is to be able to make decisions, design solutions, and create outcomes that are mutually beneficial to all invested parties. Good businesses understand this. They will not take the short-sighted route of immediate gain at the expense of their customers. The same is true with intra-organization interactions. Anytime we create solutions that work only for some, we are setting the stage for our own demise. Every revolution in history started because the leaders who put the current system in place created a system that only worked for some. Generally, these kinds of systems only work for an elite few. When this happens, inevitably the masses rise up and overthrow those in power. If we want to clear the stage of political maneuvering and power struggles so that most of our time and effort is spent solving real issues, we need to be committed to solutions that benefit all.

> If we want to clear the stage of political maneuvering and power struggles and solve real issues, we need to be committed to solutions that benefit all.

Now this does not mean it will benefit all equally all the time. We have discussed that sometimes one part of the organization must sacrifice for the good of the whole. But that sacrifice should always be in the long term interest of everyone involved or impacted by the decision.

If we go back to the disciplinary situation presented earlier, we can see how this idea was lived out. The camp benefactor who was offended by the behavior of the young men at his home was heard. Not only was he heard, he was able to speak directly to the young men and articulate his own experience. The site manager saw there were consequences to the actions and thus the culture of the camp was protected. The program manager was able to keep the two young men in meaningful roles and work with them to bring about change. The young men were able to reestablish trust and confidence in their judgment and maturity. We, as directors, had found a way to create a win-win for all parties and deliver a clear message about the importance of our policies. In the end, the boys rose to the occasion and demonstrated a great example for their peers. One will return next year in a role of higher responsibility due to his response to the situation.

Creating a Place That Works for All

All of these guiding principles which orient collaborative work have a single thing in common. They all point toward creating organizations that do not simply serve the few but enable all members to make meaningful contributions to the success of the whole. In the mid 1990s, there were a number of articles outlining successful organizational change in some of the best known companies in the world. Sears, Harley Davidson, Shell Oil, GM, GE—all made substantial moves in a positive direction. Their focus moved beyond structural changes to address individual beliefs and assumptions.

> "The most successful companies in our study recognized that behavioral change as not just an outcome of the transformation but as its driving engine. As a result, they focused attention beyond the conventional ...restructuring hierarchy and reengineering its processes, and devoted most of their attention to ... changing individual attitudes, assumptions and behaviors" (Philips, Ghoshal, & Bartlett, 1996, p. 24).

When people learned to think differently, they could contribute differently. Many of these companies also did something else that speaks to a real shift in priorities, they took the time to close the gap between the top of the organization and the bottom. The senior leaders took intentional actions to speak to and hear from their employees at all levels. GE, Sears, Harley Davidson and Shell Oil spent a good amount of time educating their members about the strategy and business model of the companies. This allowed for everyone to understand the direction and to make a different kind of contribution.

> When people learn to think differently, they contribute differently.

While this is still soaking in, let me offer you another example. In the movie *Moneyball* (De Luca, Horovitz, & Pitt, 2011), the Oakland A's general manager Billy Bean is trying to make a massive cultural change in his organization. Through a good part of the movie, he is aloof from the players and uses structural change (signing players, trading players) to effect a new mindset. He uses his "authority" to try to force the manager to go along. In the end, he begins to focus on what he can do rather than trying to force others into change. One of the key changes was his ongoing involvement with players at the individual level, teaching not only the game but, more importantly, a new mindset toward the game. His change worked because he realized he had to help players change the way they thought before he could change the way they played.

The demands of customers and the speed of change require us to have a broad knowledge of the priorities and direction of our organizations. Connecting to this bigger picture adds more meaning to the work of each contributor, they become more capable of making those contributions. Collaborative leaders invite all voices to participate in appropriate ways; such leaders understand the most important insight could come from the least likely place (Hansen, 2009). Though the concept of collaboration can be elusive to pin down, it is really not overly complicated. When people who trust each other and are committed to mutual success talk honestly and listen intently, collaboration is present. It is, however, more difficult to walk in this way for it also requires leaders, both formal and informal, to give away power in order to create influence. This requires much more courage than most leaders are able to gather. And unless we simply point to the top of the organization and pronounce judgment, we must look in the mirror. For often, we also seek self-security first and hang onto what power we have too tightly. The only way to realize a

> Connecting to the bigger picture adds more meaning to the work of each contributor.

> Important insight can come from the least likely place.

> When people who trust each other and are committed to mutual success talk honestly and listen intently, collaboration is present.

better way of working in an organization is for each member to step up and lead better from where they are.

In Case You Are Interested...

Collaboration is a subject that has been explored with many different definitions. It has been looked at from the team level and as such often resembles basic team work. Hansen (2009) takes the basic concept of working together to the next level looking at getting people in very different contexts to work together across the organization.

We suggest that collaboration is more like a collective learning process where there is an exploration of shared assumptions that can result in new understanding. This perspective first came to my attention in an article by Diane Rawlings (2000) almost two decades ago. She was looking at paradigms for executive teams who wanted to move beyond the simple model of cooperation and teamwork.

This learning perspective as a foundation for collaboration was also reflected in a number of publications focusing on dialogue (Bohm, 1996; Ellinor & Gerard, 1998; Issacs, 1999; Senge, 1990). The idea of dialogue was a quality of interaction that allowed members to become aware of their assumptions and hold the tension of their differences to produce new understanding.

Finally, this book suggests that meetings are places where small groups of people develop not only group process but individual capacity which will let them contribute in more profound ways. Kloppenborg and Petrick (1999) argue much the same perspective, seeing meetings as a place to build group character, increasing the willingness and ability for a group to act ethically. A similar perspective, that small groups are where culture is built and sustained, is echoed in a book by Olson and Eoyang (2001).

Your Workplace and Emotional Process

"For collaboration to happen, we need to first be aware
of the emotional process and have the courage to step up
and be vulnerable."

One of the limiting factors of improving human interaction within the workplace is that we in the western world have a limited view of how people learn and change. The search for a collaborative culture will require a good deal of retooling our skills of social engagement. We have been guided for the last 400 years by the idea that humans mostly make rational decisions. The Enlightenment, with its focus and value on human reason, has anchored our educational efforts squarely in the arena of conscious, cognitive, rational thought. Consequently, most of our efforts to change have been focused on the mind. If we get good information to people, provide them with clear concepts, and help them articulate clear plans, we will change people. But that is only half the equation. New research sheds light on how the brain functions, revealing that rational thought is only part of the process and the last part of the process to produce influence. Science is helping us rediscover that we are not primarily rational creatures but creatures driven by our desires, the subconscious awareness that is formed more through our bodies and emotions than rational thought. This chapter explores how this works and what the implications are for how we lead, meet, and work together.

Nearly five hundred years ago, an entrepreneurial leader starting a new religious order proposed the guiding force shaping our identities and thus our actions, was our desires. Ignatius, the founder of the Jesuit order, placed great attention on "our deepest desires, the ones that shape our lives: desires that help us know who we are to become and what we are to do" (Martin, 2010, p. 59). The philosopher, James Smith (2009), speaking to leaders in higher education emphasizes, "Our identity is shaped by what we love ... what gives us ... a sense of meaning, purpose, understanding, and orientation to our being-in-the-world ... what we think the good life looks like ...." I know what you are thinking. These are old and probably superstitious ways of understanding people and the ideas are confined to religious institutions. But science is coming back around to these "old" ideas. Researchers in the field of educational neuroscience are realizing the power of emotion on the learning process. "Our attitudes toward learning are built upon prior experiences. Our emotional responses trigger memories, recollection of information, and even subconsciously affect how we approach a task or lesson" (Stanchfield, 2014, p. 8).

You may ask, even if this is true, what difference does it make to me as an organizational leader? We need to be aware of another level of development going on all the time in our organizations that may counter or discourage the kind of collaborative behavior we talk about needing in our presentations. We present ideas about the power of collaboration but little change seems to take root. This is because members of our organization are being influenced through various practices in their daily work that may be promoting an anti-collaborative mindset. Kegan and Lahey (2009), in their book *Immunity to Change*, discuss the power of unconscious assumptions that keeps people stuck, unable to change, even when there is a deliberate effort to try to change. Why is this? If we are truly more influenced by our collection of emotional memories, automat-

> Intellectual awareness is much easier to achieve than a shift in emotional awareness and courage.

ed responses, and hidden assumptions than we are by our cognitive thoughts, then there is a deeper place of learning that has taken hold and shaped the way we see ourselves and the world around us. This deeper formation is the result of messages hidden in our stories, our images, and our practices; those things which engage our imaginations and shape our identities. "Because we are affective before we are cognitive (and even while we are cognitive), visions of good get inscribed in us by means that are commensurate with our primarily affective, imaginative nature" (Smith, 2009, p. 53). In my own research and practice (Robinson & Rose, 2004), I found that intellectual awareness was much easier to achieve than a shift in emotional awareness and courage. Our "adaptive unconscious," as Smith calls it, is a powerful force (Wilson, 2002).

So, this argument is to help you, the reader, become aware that people learn and values and practices are formed, not just from what we think and the information we hold, but by our actions and emotional make-up as well. The implication is that **how** you do work, **how** you run meetings, shapes the mindset and thus the culture of your meetings more than any content or ideas that you articulate. We will look at concrete expressions of this later in the chapter, but for now we need to realize that we cannot help people change simply by focusing on information and cognitive thoughts.

So where do we start? The place to start is to first understand emotional process and how it impacts individuals and the groups in which move. Then we can look at what kinds of organizational practices may be at work undermining our intentions to be collaborative.

Emotional Process

Emotional process is the taking in of data from our environment and responding to it (Kerr & Bowen, 1988). It is an innate action that all living things have. It is a survival process that has been honed over time. The process works like this: We scan our environment looking for threats. When we perceive a threat, we become anxious. Anxiety is a very powerful and motivating force so we take steps to get rid of the anxiety and return ourselves to a secure state. This keeps us from walking in front of cars, getting between a mother bear and her cubs, eating food covered in mold, or spending too much alone time with our in-laws. It is a natural process organized around our survival.

Humans, unlike many living things, have a very active thought life. We are shaped over time to hold certain assumptions and beliefs. We corrupt the emotional process flow, because we have learned that anything new, anything we cannot control or understand may be a threat. We "know" this because embarrassment is a bad experience. So many real opportunities to grow and learn are perceived to be threats because we may not understand them or fear we are not good at them. David Rock helps us be more precise about what causes us to feel anxious. He identifies five domains of human social experience that when threatened create a great deal of anxiety: Status, Certainty, Autonomy, Relatedness, and Fairness.

> Many real opportunities to grow and learn are perceived to be threats because we may not understand them or fear we are not good at them.

"Status is about relative importance to others. Certainty concerns being able to predict the future. Autonomy provides a sense of control over events. Relatedness is a sense of safety with others, of friend rather than foe. And fairness is a perception of fair exchanges between people" (2008, p. 1).

We find much of our personal value and security in these things. Physically, a challenge to one of these things creates the same brain process as if our lives were being threatened (Rock). When threatened, these things create strong emotional responses grounded in shame, the fear of not being good enough (Brown, 2012).

When we experience what we believe are threats to our identity and well-being we react with automated responses that we have learned over time help to restore a sense of security. These automated responses are not thought out (Friedman, 1999). They are knee-jerk responses mostly learned from when we were children. So, for me, when I was young, if I felt uncomfortable I would just withdraw and run away from the situation. Some found crying got them the response they needed to feel safe. Others found that being loud or intimidating could get them what they wanted. Unfortunately, these responses also tend to be our least effective and least creative responses to a situation. They may help us feel better but they tend to keep us trapped in an illusion of control because we avoid the discomfort of the anxiety. Yet, anxiety is not just a signal of danger but is also present in appropriate risk-taking behaviors that help us grow, mature, and become more effective.

So if we are shaped to think that anything that challenges our status, certainty, autonomy, relatedness and fairness is bad, then we will have a very difficult time being collaborative. Collaboration requires us to let go of these very things in order to be influenced by others and understand more than we could on our own. Collaboration, at an unconscious level, will be a perpetual threat to our well-being and we will undermine it at every turn regardless of what we say we believe and value. Collaboration takes an intentional emotional shift before we can engage it with our whole being.

> Collaboration takes an intentional emotional shift before we can engage it with our whole being.

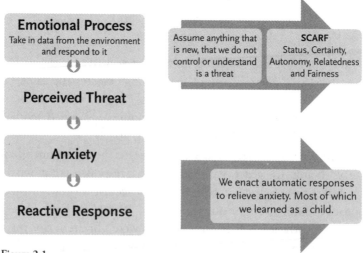

Figure 2.1

Unconscious Development

Every time we enter an interaction with others, we are guided by not only our conscious thoughts and intents but also by a whole set of unconscious beliefs that define what Smith (2009) calls the "good life." This idea of the good life is an image of what we aspire to obtain, keep, and protect in terms of status, influence, security and affluence. It tells us when we have arrived. The real challenge is that most of what defines this good-life image is developed beyond the elements of conscious, rational thought. It has been forming in us our whole lives and is a mixture of assumptions, emotional memories, values, subliminal messages, and automatic behaviors.

We talked in the previous section about how automatic behaviors get formed through our emotional process. The other components—assumptions, emotional memories, and subliminal messages—find their way into us through practices or rituals and images (Smith, 2009). We develop this unconscious set of beliefs and meanings through bodily learning rather than rational thought. It is not that rational thought cannot influence our unconscious beliefs but our embodied learning through ritual practices and visual images generally comes first and is learned much quicker than rational thought. So if we are going to truly impact the maturity and effectiveness of our teams, we must understand what is being communicated at the unconscious or embodied level and what images are already embedded in the minds of our members.

> If we are going to impact the maturity and effectiveness of our teams, we must understand what is being communicated at the unconscious or embodied level and what images are already embedded in the minds of our members.

Let me try to illustrate what I am talking about. You walk into a conference room furnished with a long table surrounded by chairs. There are single chairs at each end but only one is occupied, the one nearest the front of the room. When we enter the room, what assumptions are we already making about the person in that chair even if we know nothing about the person? Most likely we are assuming this is a person of influence, power, and authority. Why would we make that assumption? Well, in most situations the person at the head of the table is the leader. In many families who still eat dinner at the table, the parents tend to sit at the ends of the table. This is our first education about table etiquette. No one had to tell us this as children. We learned it through the ritual practice of daily meals. Members of our organizations have a number of beliefs that are taught and reinforced, not by rational messages, but through the rituals of work and the images at work and in society.

> A number of beliefs are taught and reinforced, not by rational messages, but through the rituals of work and the images at work and in society.

Let's consider the typical staff meeting. We have all set through dozens or hundreds of these. Many staff meetings are a combination of messages from the leader and updates from the members of the staff. The arrangement of the room has the leader as a focal point at the center or the head of the table with the staff situated around the table. After some introductory remarks, the meeting is fully engaged with each member taking his or her turn to talk about what is happening in his or her area. The members provide the status on projects, priorities for the week, and unavoidable problems or setbacks with which they are dealing. The unspoken goals in the room are to

1) present oneself as busy, effective, and in control;
2) to avoid delivering bad news whenever possible; and
3) to avoid embarrassment which could be caused by being unprepared or ineffective.

As mentioned earlier, all of this is to protect one's status, certainty, and autonomy in particular; however, it also impacts the relational dynamics and perceived fairness in the group. There is also the assumed goals of protecting one's influence and seat at the table as well as the reputation and influence of your department and by extension your department's leader. Now where in our training, orientation programs, and handbooks are these goals taught and reinforced? What incentives are required to ensure that members consistently accomplish these goals? And yet without clear articulation or intentional monetary reinforcement, every person in every staff meeting is typically able to achieve these goals year after year. How does this happen?

It happens because we are formed as much by the images we see, the stories we tell, and the rituals we experience as we are by any propositional truth we are told or taught. This level of formation is deep. From our parents, to our schools, to a myriad of images we see in media, we are taught compliance is good and disruption is bad. We are taught that it is better to get permission before acting. These lessons are so ingrained that they guide our actions long after we may have learned to think in alternative ways.

> We are formed as much by the images we see, the stories we tell, and the rituals we experience as we are by any propositional truth we are told or taught.

I once worked with an IT group that was trying to create a culture of empowerment, self-management, and personal responsibility. The leaders were clear, the resources were available, and the messages were consistent. Yet it took many months for the workers in this group to believe it was true and start operating with the freedom that had been given them. Their new world was so much different than the image that was formed in them that they literally could not believe it to be true in the beginning. They often waited for direction rather than taking initiative. It took the manager mandating that all had to use their fifteen days of training each year before they actually would take it. Many did not realize they had within their power to determine which roles they could play in the organization based on how they used their training to develop the necessary skill sets.

So you may ask, what does a positive, formative practice or ritual look like? How can we help people learn from an embodied ritual how to be collaborative? In my work with organizations, I typically help them install an **action-learning process** (Robinson, 2005) as a way to practice the mind-set and skills to collaborate while maintaining high levels of personal responsibility. In the action-learning process (see Table 2.1), a presenter brings an issue they are trying to solve to the group. The group starts by asking questions to fully understand the issue and to make sure the presenter is solving the right issue. With

Table 2.1 Summary of Differences Between an Informational Meeting (Staff Meeting) and a Collaborative Problem-Solving Meeting (Action Learning)

	Typical Staff Meeting	Action Learning
Focus of Power	Leader or boss	Presenter or person asking for help
Goal of the Meeting	• Deliver good news • Share information • Present self as busy and productive	• Solve a challenging issue • Let others help you frame and understand the issue • Use shared intelligence of the group to better understand issues and options
Role of the Leader	• Evaluate • Set priorities • Motivate workers to work harder • Arbitrate what is good news	• Facilitate open conversation • Keep the group disciplined to the action-learning process • Empower others to take action
Values Enacted in the Ritual	• Be right • Be productive • Be strong • Be certain	• Be open • Be collaborative • Be disciplined • Be respectful

the guidance of the presenter, the group will settle on the core issue to be resolved and will then start generating options or solutions to the issue. The presenter, with this input, chooses actions to take. They go out, take action, and circle back around to let the group know how it worked out so all can learn from the experience.

This action-learning process is a completely different ritual than a typical staff meeting. For instance, the power in the meeting is possessed by the person who is taking responsibility for an issue. The interactions are guided by asking questions rather than making statements and by respecting the ability of the person to take care of his or her own business. The focus is not on being right but on asking for help and initiating trust. This process embodies a completely different image of successful meetings and collaboration. The groups I have worked with tell me it changes not only how they solve problems but also how they interact in all their meetings. They tend to listen better, ask more questions, and offer suggestions without being offended if they are not accepted.

> Action learning changes not only how groups solve problems but also how they interact in all their meetings.

Conclusion

What limits our ability to collaborate, even when we are intentionally talking about the fact that it is needed, is our anxiety. Anxiety of the individuals and the collective anxiety of the group both cause us to be reactive, defensive, passive, and controlling. The more we act in this way the more we signal that we cannot trust each other. For collaboration to happen, we need to first be aware of the emotional process (amount of anxiety and its influence on the current interaction) and have the courage to step up and be vulnerable. This is an ability that we can practice. We can improve this both individually and collectively, but we first have to recognize the critical element that limits our success. Paradoxically, the key to good collaboration is mature individuals who through a process of self-definition become clear about what they believe, courageous in their willingness to engage others, and intentional about how they deal with difference.

> The key to good collaboration is mature individuals who through a process of self-definition become clear about what they believe, courageous in their willingness to engage others, and intentional about how they deal with difference.

A recent Deloitte report (2016) points to organizations turning to cross-functional teams as the core element of their organizational designs. These are small groups who form around key tasks, objectives, or projects and disband when their work is done. There will be pressure on these teams to form quickly, learn deeply, and collaborate deliberately if they are to be successful. These teams, powered by cultures that promote engagement, will push organizations forward.

This is not fully a new topic. These trends have been around. The issue is that we still are not making the kind of progress that will be needed. Collaboration will not be solved nor created with surface oriented techniques of human interaction. Collaboration and innovation call for clear minds and mature character, both of which are undermined by the often unnoticed scourge in organizations, anxiety. As we discussed earlier, brain research tells us when we feel threatened, we focus on security not innovation. We can change structures and attempt to shape cultures but until we have a set of leaders at all levels who have the character and capacity to be purposeful, though they may be anxious, we won't create anything that can last. This calls for deep levels of awareness, self-awareness, where we understand our own triggers—the triggers that exist in our teams and thus our organizations—and can explore the deep-seated but unchallenged assumptions that keep us seeing threats around every corner. Though many will attempt to tackle this through cleverly designed experiences with the best information, this is not a dilemma that can be thought into. Thinking is a part of sustaining the progress but it starts with courage, transparency, listening, and the willingness to forgo actions that will keep us protected in order to engage actions that might enliven us all. We will not defeat the infection of anxiety by keeping out the pathogens. Rather, we must enhance the immune system to develop mature leaders at all levels who can resist the damaging effects of uncertainty and lack of control as we empower each other to bring to the table the best of what we have.

> Collaboration takes courage, transparency, listening, and the willingness to forgo actions that keep us protected in order to engage actions that might enliven us all.

In Case You Are Interested...

Though there is overlap and similarities with Emotional Intelligence (EI), the foundational theory for this work comes from Bowen Family Systems Theory. Bowen (1966, 1976, 1978, 1988) understood the family as an emotional system with the underlying driver being anxiety. His theory contained eight core ideas, of which self-differentiation, triangles and emotional cutoff are prominent in this work. Edwin Friedman (1985, 1999), a student of Bowen extended the ideas of the family emotional unit to leaders and organizations. Bowen Theory is considered one of the best researched theories in the family therapy field due to its strong grounding in biological science. Emotional systems theory extends EI ideas of self-awareness, self-regulation (key components of self-differentiation) and social awareness from the interpersonal relationships to the functioning of systems. This relates the ideas that reflect the complexity and amplification of relational networks and how emotion in the system impacts individuals beyond just individual awareness and choice. Key ideas here include sabotage, triangles, and forces of individuation and togetherness. There have been a couple validated instruments to study the key concepts of Bowen theory including the work of Skowron and Friedlander (1998) and Dickenson, et al. (1996).

Emotional Intelligence, though not the theoretical foundation of this book has a number of findings that support and help explain the dynamics discussed here. Goleman (1985) popularized the idea of EI (Kunnanatt, 2008) with his competency based model. EI has been tied to many benefits in organizations and is thus a well-documented concept. Mishra and Mohapatra (2009) provide an excellent summary of the various streams of EI research, organizing them into three threads: Ability models (Salovey & Mayer (1990), Mixed and/or Ability models (Bar-On, 1997), and Personality Models (Goleman, 1998; Cherniss & Goleman 2001). Both EI and Bowen Theory advocate and substantiate the critical role emotion plays in shaping human behavior and group dynamics.

Brain research supports the ideas of the role of emotion, and in particular anxiety, in the functioning and decision-making of the brain. Steimer (2002) provides a very nice overview of the research with a particular look to the reactive nature of behavior in response to anxiety states. Though there is some debate as to the level of direct causation emotion plays with behavior (Baumeister, Vohs, DeWall, & Zhang, 2007) there does appear to be a relationship between emotion, cognitive functioning, and behavior.

A final theoretical concept foundational to this chapter is the role of non-conscious cognitive functioning in our formational development. Smith (2009) builds off the work of Wilson (2002) to identify an alternative explanation for behavior. Rather than being highly rational creatures who thoughtfully decide our every action, we are beings who are driven by desire or as Smith says the image of the "Good Life." Wilson's term is the adaptive unconscious. Both are referring to deeply held beliefs, assumptions, and emotional memories which shape not only our behavior but what we attend to and the meanings we make of our experience that operate typically out of our consciousness. It is this out of sight operating system that holds our identities and understanding of the world which shapes how we interpret input from the world and thus influences both our emotion and behavior. Wilson indicates that emotion and behavior are the tangible manifestations of the adaptive unconscious, and as such, are the pathways to understanding what we might hold to be true. Both of the current researchers echo the writings of Ignatius who saw emotion as the pathway to understanding our true beliefs and shaping the direction of our lives (Lowney, 2003).

Heron (1992) provides a helpful distinction when it comes to emotion that points to what the adaptive unconscious may be trying to answer for us. Heron sees emotion as a response to an individual's encounter with his or her own needs, whether they are being met or not. Feelings are social manifestations of emotional, physiological experiences with things like empathy and sympathy being examples. If this is true, the emotional process may be focused on finding answers to those deepest held needs, such as those outlined in Maslow's model (1943) or Rock's SCARF model (2008).

CHAPTER THREE

Self-Definition as a Leadership Practice

"Self-definition is an ongoing, life-long process whereby we
come to gain clarity about what we value, what we do, why
we do things, and what makes us valuable."

When it comes to leadership (i.e., intentional influence), most people give away their most critical source of power. Too often the focus is on how to get other people to be the way the leader desires them to be. It is really not surprising since most leadership theories focus our attention toward others and how we get other people to do what we want. If we have any hope of promoting and sustaining our ability to collaborate, we must understand that in any given social situation, the only person we can change is ourselves. Thus "All leadership begins with self-leadership, and self-leadership begins with knowing oneself" (Lowney, 2003, p. 98).

Before we go deeper into self-awareness and how we develop this insight, we need to understand why this is important in the context of a team or organizational system. When people come together, we come with various assumptions, fears, ambitions, and values. We form emotional systems, which involve some level of anxiety. When these systems are healthy, they manage the anxiety. Yet, often, these systems are anxious and that anxiety limits clearness of thought, purposeful action, and innovation. When anxiety is not managed, people revert to automated behaviors that seek control and thus security within the system. People become reactive to each other, and in the end, the ability to perform well breaks down. Leaders in these systems can have a great impact if they are a non-anxious presence. Such leaders can dissipate the escalating anxiety and help the group return to a calmer place, where the proverbial "cooler heads prevail." In addition, mature leaders (or self-defined leaders) foster conditions that do two important things:

1) promote maturity and self-definition in others, and
2) reduces chronic stress and anxiety.

Chronic anxiety is created when there are secrets, a lack of transparency, mismanaged boundaries, lack of direction and/or an overall lack of fairness. Self-defined leaders create conditions where these types of things are not permitted to exist.

So, what exactly is self-defined leadership? The self-defined leader can 1) manage their own anxiety in the face of others, 2) think for themselves and take a stand regardless of how others may respond, and 3) stay connected to others but emotionally separate (Friedman, 1999). The way this is manifested is that self-defined leaders have clear values that guide their decisions. They have the courage to evaluate their own actions and even learn from failures. They can tell others the truth even if it is hard to hear. They can take positions that are necessary even if they are not popular. They are purposeful and not reactive to others, especially those who are different from them. They ask the hard questions because they are not afraid of the answers. They can entertain ideas very different from their own in the hope of new insight. In essence, self-defined leaders possess a level of maturity, courage, and humility that helps them remain calm in the midst of stress. They invest in developing this maturity in everyone around them even if that means someone more influential may rise. They can collaborate because they are not afraid to change, to be influenced, or to be vulnerable. This focus gets us to the core of why so many teams and organizations cannot succeed.

> Self-defined leaders can collaborate because they are not afraid to change, to be influenced, or to be vulnerable.
>
> Self-defined leaders possess a level of maturity, courage, and humility that brings calm in the midst of stress.

They lack the capacity and character for meaningful contribution. Self-defined leaders change those dynamics.

Before we move to some strategies for becoming a self-defined leader, I want to offer one more milestone to help us know if we are moving on the right path. A key question is to ask, "Why am I doing what I am doing?" If there is a sense, even if it is small, that you are doing what you are doing to change another person rather than yourself, you are missing the point.

> If you are doing what you are doing to change another person rather than yourself, you are missing the point.

Here is an example: I worked with a co-facilitator many years ago. She was well meaning but she came in unprepared and that made for a rough day. After a talk with my boss, I knew I had to talk to her about it. Now I am not one for confrontation so just thinking about this conversation made me very anxious, but it needed to be done. So I pressed in and set up the meeting. Why was I going to have this conversation? Was there some potential benefit to my colleague? Yes, but this was about changing me. It was moving me from being a victim. It was going to make me press through my anxiety and thus build some emotional stamina. It was an opportunity for me to do what I believed to be right rather than what was easy. We had the talk, and I was honest and straightforward. As I left her office she began to cry, though it was not for the reason I assumed. She told me no one had ever valued her enough to tell her the truth and she thanked me. As I look at that interaction now, I realize it included many things that I would come to believe about what mature leaders do. They first make choices based on what they believe rather than what is expedient. They are willing to be vulnerable and thus trust that many people given the right circumstances will rise to the occasion. And they make space for people to make their own choices rather than assume what another person may do, think, or say. This is not only the way we live as a self-defined person but also how we help those around us do the same.

Strategies for Self-Definition

How do we become more mature, more self-defined? Self-definition is an ongoing, lifelong process whereby we come to gain clarity about what we value, what we do, why we do things and what makes us valuable. Since the foundation of our maturity (i.e., ability to self-define or differentiate) is below our level of consciousness, we cannot simply think our way to maturity. There is a place for thoughtful consideration and determination but information and technique alone will not change our maturity level (Friedman, 1999). The sort of change we are talking about requires us to surface and challenge our deepest-held assumptions. To do so we must develop a high level of emotional awareness as well as the stamina to be uncomfortable and not react to achieve certainty and security. This kind of learning and development requires the discipline of reflection on experience. So, back to the question, how do we learn to do this?

Our deepest assumptions, particularly those that define what Smith (2009) called the image of the good life, are often buried deep. Yes, assumptions are a thinking element but often we have to access those indirectly in order to gain real understanding. So for me, I have come to see that we must use other parts of our lives to piece who we are together. We are all made up of a triangle of factors that can be used to understand who we are. The elements of the triangle are 1) what we think, 2) what we feel, and 3) what we do.

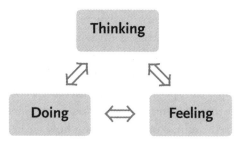

Because our deepest assumptions are not easily accessible, we must learn to use things that are more immediate to us. These are feelings and actions. **Feelings** have a physical expression. When fear sets in, our hearts race, our hands sweat, and our stomachs get tight. Now, feelings are often given a bad rap because we can feel things that are not actually supported by reality. We can fear things that are not really in existence but are only potential. However, feelings are very good at revealing to us what we really believe in the moment. Consequently, if we listen to what we feel/experience inside, and begin to ask some key questions, we have the opportunity to discover an assumption we might not have known we possessed. Additionally, we generally feel things when something important is happening to us. So, if we learn to listen to what is happening within us, we have a path to self-discovery.

We can also use an alertness to emotion to understand others. Now we cannot know, without checking, what specific emotion a person is experiencing. However, we can observe if there is the presence of emotion. We can often tell if it is positive or negative. We can often discern if it is intense or not. And equipped with the understanding that emotion is only present when important things are happening, we can get curious and help others explore what they are experiencing by asking a few questions. We will talk more about those questions in a moment.

The second element available to us, if we want to really understand what we believe and what drives our actions, is our **behavior**. Again, what we do has a physical manifestation and thus is observable. Now we should realize that there is often a gap between what we do and what we say; however, we always do what we really believe. Like our emotions, our actions are driven by deeply held logics, beliefs that form desires and thus generate actions. When we are purposeful in reflecting on our actions, we can discover why we do what we do. When we understand why we do what we do, we have the opportunity to change at a deep and sustainable level.

As is true with individuals, teams and groups can also use reflection on experience to discern what the group believes, values,

> When we understand why we do what we do, we have the opportunity to change at a deep and sustainable level.

> With reflection and awareness, come the ability to challenge assumptions, clarify values, and purposefully align with a healthier desire.

and desires. With reflection and awareness, comes the ability to challenge assumptions, clarify values, and purposefully align what we do to a better desire, a desire that is more healthy and supportive of the long-term benefit of all.

Now that we know feelings and actions can tell us a lot about ourselves and each other, how do we actually use experience to create understanding? In any experience, we have action or non-action (which can be just as important), and we have emotion along with some level of **thinking**. It is important to note that the more tired, anxious, or stressed we are, the less our thinking plays a meaningful role in what we do. This is true, unless we are intentional. The discipline of reflection helps us become more intentional. I would like to say before we move on, the most powerful impact of reflection might just be that it forms us to make sense of our experience in an intentional way.

> The more tired, anxious, or stressed we are, the less our thinking plays a meaningful role in what we do.
>
> The most powerful impact of reflection might just be that it allows us to make sense of our experience in an intentional way.

Although the content of what we discuss, write, or think has some utility, forming the habit of reflecting in order to really understand our experience is the more important orientation.

So take any experience that you have and start by asking a couple of simple questions—**What did I feel?** and **What did I do?** That will get you started. I should also say, the experiences that are easiest to learn from are those where the emotion was strong and/or the consequences of our actions were painful. It is possible to learn from success but it is much harder. Pain, discomfort and disappointment grab our attention in a unique way.

Now that we have named feelings and actions, we can take the next step. We should ask ourselves, of all the things that I could have felt or done, why did I feel or do what I did? In any given experience, there are a multitude of options for us but we take specific action or feel specific things because of what we believe. Our assumptions shape our choices without us really being aware of it. So, if we ponder why we did what we did, we can begin to discern what assumptions are guiding us. Our first answers will likely yield the first level of assumptions. These are the assumptions we make about ourselves, others, and the way the world works to fill in the gaps of our

> We are sense-making creatures and if there is a gap in our information we fill it in with assumptions.

knowledge. We are sense-making creatures, and if there is a gap in our information, we fill it in with assumptions (Bushe, 2009). This is why our reactions to others can seem out of proportion. We listen to each other more from memory than in the moment. Those memories, often tied to strong emotional experiences, are formed into assumptions which give us a feeling of certainty about the world around us. We can easily tell when these unchecked, memory laden assumptions are in operation because our language is generally absolute and extreme. "He always does this." "She was completely out of control." These are observations that are often powered by untested assumptions formed by previous history or encounters.

Now awareness at this level can be very helpful. It can help us make different choices, make room for people to be different, and suspend our judgments in order to gain new perspective and understanding. Over time, we can change our way of responding and acting in the world. But if we dare to ask the next level of questions, we might be able to bring into the light our desires, our vision of the good life, those things that give us a sense of value or not, which go right to the heart of maturity. So, if we want to step to another level, we should ask ourselves questions like:

1) What do my actions, feelings, and assumptions tell me about what I believe makes me safe, valuable, deserving of belonging?

Or use the SCARF model (Rock, 2008) mentioned in the previous chapter and ask questions like:

2) What did my behavior or feeling tell me about what I believe about my status?

3) How was my certainty challenged?

4) What do my actions tell me about what I believe about autonomy or fairness?

5) What do my actions tell me about what makes me acceptable or establishes my relatedness to others?

These questions are getting to the heart of who we are—why we do what we do. It is our assumed but unchallenged vision of the good life that actually shapes what we pay attention to and the kinds of options that are available to us in solving our problems. We tend to see things that confirm what we believe, and we ignore those things that challenge what we believe. Thus, if we cannot challenge our deepest held beliefs, we will just not see things we should be seeing. If I believe vulnerability is weakness and weakness makes me unacceptable, I will never risk the vulnerability of asking for help. If I cannot open myself up to help—admit that I may not be right—then I will never be able to collaborate.

> If we cannot challenge our deepest held beliefs, we will not see things we should be seeing.

Sustaining Self-Defined Perspective

Listening inward is the beginning of self-awareness. Asking good questions will lead us to a clear sense of what we believe and why we do what we do. But to sustain a life perspective that reflects the maturity of a self-defined leader, we need something to orient and ground us. At the heart of this process is wrestling with our view of our own value. Self-defined leaders realize their value is innate. It is a gift that we all received at birth. Our value is not determined by productivity, possessions, status, popularity, or power. If the answer to the question, "What makes me valuable?" is any of the items in this list, we will not make it very far down the path of self-definition. We will inevitably be distracted by the need to do something to prove our value. When we do this, we

> At the heart of the process is wrestling with our view of our own value. Self-defined leaders realize their value is innate.

become emotionally attached to a particular outcome or response by others. When this happens, our efforts will move away from getting the best ideas and understanding into our conversations, and we will strive to convince, convert, or defeat those who disagree with us. This is the ultimate state that defies collaboration.

Ignatius, the founder of the Jesuit order, emphasized the idea of emotional indifference as the key to effective work. Collaboration requires a certain level of flexibility and agility to join in and reform our positions as we come to new insights. We cannot do this if we are emotionally tied to a certain answer. "Only by becoming indifferent—free of prejudices and attachments and therefore, free to choose any course of action—do [people] become strategically flexible" (Lowney, 2003, p. 97). This does not mean we have no values or we do not care, instead we are emotionally open to the fact that things can manifest in ways we could not imagine on our own. We do not assume the certainty of our answers. This allows us to step back and gain a broader perspective on what is possible and even how we might improve if we just accept the input of others.

> Self-defined leaders are emotionally open to the fact that things can manifest in ways they could not imagine on their own.

The ability to step back emotionally and examine ideas, actions, and motives requires maturity—a sense of knowing and valuing who you are. Without a sense of value, such considerations are too threatening to our sense of self. Brown (2012) helps us understand that the courage to be vulnerable and set healthy boundaries, both of which are imperative for collaboration, has a connection to shame. "Shame is the intensely painful feeling or experience of believing that we are flawed and therefore unworthy of love and belonging" (p. 69). The belief that we only have value if our context or important people around us give it to us keeps us trapped in fear. When we are afraid, we avoid or coerce the acceptance we need from others. In Brown's research, the only difference between those who lived in fear and shame and those who lived "whole-heartedly" was that whole-hearted people believed they were worthy of love and acceptance—that they had value.

The self-defined leader will recognize this clarity of our value is not a onetime event. It is a lifelong project in which we continually fight against the voices that say we are not enough. Self-defined leaders learn they are at their best when they are confident in their value. They are less afraid, more able to give others respect, to listen to perspectives far from their own, and to be patient as those around them work their way toward new understanding. When they are lost and not at their best, they circle back to ask questions about what they are believing at the moment about their value and its source.

Beyond this personal sense of value and acceptance, self-defined leaders give away what they have received. They are purposeful at reminding others that they also have an innate value that makes them a meaningful contributor. This is often accomplished without words. Making space for others to speak their mind, being open to their questions,

> Self-defined leaders are purposeful at reminding others they also have an innate value that makes them a meaningful contributor.

being vulnerable and humble about what we think we know—all communicate a value in the person or people with whom we are interacting. When we can do this, we can focus on the real problem at hand rather than use the problem we are attempting to solve as a gladiator arena where we can prove our worth by getting our ideas accepted by others. We stop posturing and enter into meaningful conversation where our various perspectives are heard and understood, where new meaning can arise from shared understanding, and we can see solutions that are often hidden from us in our scramble of self-serving positioning.

I was once in an action-learning session in a Fortune 500 energy company that included a young lady who was just out of college. At each meeting she was very pleasant and participated in the conversations, yet, she never brought an issue of her own to the group. After about three months of this, I decided to investigate. At first, she deflected my questions and remained positive. Then, she just broke into tears. The group's first reaction was to calm her down because we were all uncomfortable with her distress. I actually saw them start to stand up and go to her and then remember what we had talked about in the training process. So, instead of trying to quickly relieve the crying, they sat with her in the distress. They made room for her to reveal something important about herself to the group. After a bit, she stopped crying and was able to tell us that she was greatly pressured in her upbringing not to make mistakes. She thought her job was to be perfect at work. As we talked more about her perspective, it came to the forefront that being perfect and not making mistakes was a part of what she believed made her valuable. The group now had a common issue and we explored the idea of personal value and the source of that value. This group had come face-to-face with an aspect of one person's definition of the good life, at least at work. We had the chance to challenge that assumption and bring her into the group where she could more fully participate.

Tactics of Self-Defined Leaders

Equipped with a clear sense of self that provides the courage to engage with others in a truly collaborative way, self-defined leaders can create an environment that invites others into the same mindset. There are three key tactics or practices that enable leaders to set the stage for collaboration. These are presence, distance, and direction.

> Presence, distance and direction are three key tactics used to set the stage for collaboration.

Presence

As we have discussed, anxiety is the most active enemy of collaboration. When we are scared, worried, or stressed our bodies and brains limit effective interaction because we are always searching for the quickest way to feel secure. So, this is where we start as self-defined leaders. How do we combat anxiety? We become a non-anxious presence. This presence starts with an awareness that one of our most important

> One of our most important contributions is not what we can make happen but the atmosphere we create.

contributions is not what we can make happen, but rather the atmosphere we can create.

"Despite their experience, most parents, managers and mentors (teachers, therapists and consultants) have not learned this lesson. They still believe that they can teach, motivate, and inculcate values in their charges by exerting enough will, without the due regard for the natural forces that work against such well-meaning efforts but which, as with the sailor and the physician, can be harnessed to the leader's helm" (Friedman, 1999, p. 285).

What makes the self-defined leader so unusual and effective is that he or she has learned that we cannot force others to change. Force, information, or technique will not yield what the collaborative leader most desires: trust. So how do we influence those around us especially if we need to set the path? We need, as Friedman suggests above, to understand the forces at work and counter them in a way that invites responsibility, trust, and contribution from others.

"Part of the difficulty in making the conceptual leap from action to presence is that all leaders, parents, or presidents have been trained to do, that is to fix, something" (Friedman, 1999). However, the self-defined leader is aware of and focused on something more important. Being a non-anxious presence means that we can remain calm in the midst of the anxiety of others. Our influence is indirect. Rather than fix things for others, and thus play the hero that rescues and consequently weakens others, the non-anxious presence models for others the patience, calm, and courage that are required to put down the anxiety in the room. And far from being passive, the non-anxious presence can demonstrate an attitude of openness and call others (challenge) to a better place.

> Our influence is indirect. The non-anxious presence models for others the patience, calm and courage that are required to put down the anxiety in the room.

Let me give you an example. I was in a meeting where we had to deliver some disappointing news to leaders of our organization. Some budget shortfalls and other demands had emerged that were going to force us to think creatively with staffing strategies. As soon as the first details of the need for change were spoken, one member erupted in an emotionally-laden attack. He got loud, accusatory, and could not hear anything other than his own panic. Interestingly, there was some technique and information used to try to disarm the situation. The director named what was going on, specifically reaction mode, and tried to complete his explanation. This had little effect. Meanwhile, four other leaders in the meeting were not responding in kind but waiting patiently to engage differently. After a while, the energy of the eruption subsided and those who were able to remain calm began looking at the situation from various perspectives. One leader, a peer to the manager who erupted, calmly stated his reaction and advocated that he would think from the enterprise perspective, but part of that role was to also protect his area so they could deliver what was needed to make the organization effective. Notice, that due to his ability to stay calm, he could both be vulnerable (think from an enterprise perspective in a way that might cost him something) and set clear boundaries (I must advocate and protect my department) at the same time. As the anxiety subsided, new ideas began to emerge and possible options to the situation came to the surface.

Who we are in a situation is more important than what we know or what we can do. The self-defined leader is the person in the room who can be a non-anxious presence. This presence is not determined by position. It is available to any who are in the room. When our presence resists being overwhelmed by anxiety, we can find our way to a level of discussion where we all hear each other, where our difference of perspective challenges our thinking, and where people can bring forward the best of who they are. I just want to reiterate, we cannot be such a presence if we do not possess a level of self-awareness that both experiences situations and at the same time makes sense of situations, simultaneously allowing us to choose a response rather than simply react in the moment.

> Who we are in a situation is more important than what we know or what we can do.

Distance

A second consideration for the self-defined leader is the matter of distance. In human systems, if a person is too close or too far away, the result is the same—increased anxiety. What do we mean by too close? This can be a physical presence but often it means that we are too emotionally invested in how other people around us operate. We need them to be a certain way in order for us to feel secure. So we involve ourselves in their work and interactions in a way that is invasive. We call these people micro-managers. Leaders who are too close, who seek to ease their anxiety via control. The problem is such leaders try to control all manner of small things while often avoiding big things. The more they try to control it all, the more anxiety they create in the team and thus the more control they feel is necessary. So the pattern is reinforced.

> In human systems, if a person is too close or too far away, the result is the same—increased anxiety.

I was once on a wilderness trip that was a leadership development process for a group of emerging leaders. As part of the trip, each person took a turn as leader of the day. The responsibilities of the leader were to navigate (so they had map and compass), set time-lines for coming and going, and monitor the health and state of the group so as to take needed breaks. One of the participants demonstrated the invasive behavior of a micro-manager when it was his turn to lead. The first thing he did was give away his main role, placing the map and compass in the hands of other participants. Though he did not have the tools given to him to navigate, he constantly tried to micro-manage the situation. At one point, a member broke a shoelace. As he was fixing the lace, this leader came over and tried to take charge of the repair. He avoided his real job (navigation) for fear of being wrong, and over-controlled the simple things in an attempt to demonstrate control and thus value.

The opposite end of the spectrum can be just as damaging. Some people manage their emotional discomfort and anxiety by being too distant. Such leaders are always gone or, when they are in, their door is shut. Avoiding contact with people helps us not feel the tension in the relationships but it does nothing to fix it. Here is a simplistic example that illustrates the issue of being too far away. As an experiential facilitator, I use a variety of activities requiring blindfolds. When I am very quiet in these activities, group members will frequently ask if I am still there. Why do they do this? My presence does not help them see what they cannot see nor do I help them solve their dilemma. It seems just knowing that someone is there calms their anxiety and allows them to work.

The key of distance for the self-defined leader is be able to manage distance in relation to others. Too close and we do for others what they should do for themselves. Too far away and people feel abandoned and left adrift. Again, this ties in nicely with our first tactic of Presence. We need to have the appropriate distance to allow people to work and even struggle while also providing a non-anxious presence in the situation. Thus the rule of thumb is the more stressed a situation is, the more present a leader needs to be. This is not to do for others but to communicate a confidence in their abilities and a belief they can work it out.

> The appropriate distance provides a non-anxious presence while allowing people to work or even struggle in the situation.

The same is true for teams. When teams have a conflict, the instinctual response is often to avoid gathering due to the feared level of stress. This almost always leads to making assumptions because we have a lack of information and our minds fill in the blanks. The key is to lean into the conflict, face it, understand it, and identify each member's contribution to the situation and what they could do to make it better.

Direction

The final concern to monitor is direction. Direction is a way of thinking about the amount of will we are trying to impose on others. The truth is that when we pursue people in an attempt to change them, their first response is to run away even if we are right. This also shows up in how we help others solve problems. One of the reasons it is so difficult to ask for help is that we fear that others will take over the problem and impose their answer on our situation. This is a mismanagement of boundaries. Collaboration requires that we invite others into our issues for perspective and possible solutions but it is dependent on everyone allowing the right person to own the issue. When direction is off balance, we tend to impose, coerce, and convert others to our preferred way.

The worst case scenario is that when we impose or take over, we can teach people to be victims. A victim requires others to change so they can feel well. The problem is, once you teach this helplessness, trying to change it only drives people deeper into their victimhood.

So what is the appropriate way to manage direction? The key is to always promote and empower personal responsibility. We can be bold—ask hard questions and/or name situations that need attention. The difference is that we are inviting people to a choice point, a cross-road, and then allowing them to make their own decisions. We can also set our own boundaries, which communicates what we will or will not do. Allowing others to coerce us does not foster maturity either. We know we are managing direction well when those around us are seeing their part in the issue and taking responsibility for things they should own.

> Self-defined leaders invite people to a choice point, a cross-road, and then allow them to make their own decisions.

In Case You Are Interested...

Self-differentiation is a key concept of this chapter. This is one of Bowen's eight concepts and is significant in the theory presented in this book. Self-differentiation is related to emotional intelligence (EI) competencies of self-awareness and self-regulation. It is a maturation process that allows individuals to encounter difference, experience strong emotion, and still be intentional with their choices. Bowen theorists (Friedman 1999, Steinke, 1993, 2006; Kerr & Bowen, 1988) focused a great deal on emotional awareness and self-regulation being the core of differentiation. Robinson (Robinson & Rose, 2004) suggests a model for differentiation that combines both the emotional maturation of Bowen Theory and EI with the critical reflection theories defined by writers such as Mezirow (1998, 1991), Brookfield (1987), Argyris and Schon (1974), and Cranton (1994) who suggest the key to transformation and indeed sustainable change is the growing awareness of and challenging of our assumptions. With the work of Wilson (2002), it is not fully clear as to how the cognitive and the emotional work together but there does appear to be a relationship. Robinson has posited that emotion triggers automatic and reactive behavior as suggested by Friedman (1999) and Kerr and Bowen (1988) but that it is our assumptions about who we are, how the world works and what are potential threats, that shape an interpretation of the world that generates particular emotional responses.

There have been numerous studies looking at differentiation (Johnson, Buboltz & Seemann, 2003; Murdock & Gore, 2004; Skowron, 2004; Skowron & Dendy, 2004; Skowron, Wester & Azen, 2004) which provide support for the concept of self-differentiation and link it to reduction of anxiety and increased functioning in the presence of anxiety.

Other researchers and practitioners have tied the utility of emotional awareness with deep reflection on associated assumptions to stimulate meaningful change (Kegan & Lahey, 2009 & 2016; Tang & Joiner, 2006).

Looking Outward: Moving From Self-Awareness to Other-Awareness

"The goal is to develop the ability to listen to process
(how people are acting) and the content (what they are
talking about) at the same time."

We begin our practice of self-definition by listening inward and learning to be attuned to what we feel, what we think, and the underlying desires forming our actions in the world. But this is only the first step. The next step is to start looking outward so we can see and make sense of the dynamics of other people and groups. We must build some proficiency here so we can become fully aware of our context. Knowing oneself is important; however, we live in a context where other people are interacting. Our ability to positively contribute to the systems we are a part of will rely on how well we pay attention to and understand the dynamics at hand.

At this stage of developing other-awareness, we are not really seeking to intervene. We are simply practicing the ability to see the dynamics at hand. There are two key abilities we need to develop at this point:

1) See the presence of anxiety and understand its impact.
2) Listen to both the content of interactions and the process of the interaction.

As we have discussed, anxiety is a powerful influencer of human behavior. It is present in most situations, though often as an empowering force rather than a debilitating force. We want to learn to see when anxiety in other people is making them reactive and defensive and thus keeping them from fully engaging in the work at hand.

Meeting Reviews

Meetings are some of the best places to learn what to look for and interpret the dynamics among people. In a meeting, we have all the needed elements for substantial dynamics. The meeting needs to include problems to be solved and/or decisions to be made. Update or status meetings do not provide a depth of interaction necessary to see dynamics rise to the surface.

One of the key dynamics to watch for is the presence of reactive and collaborative responses. Reactive responses are generally knee-jerk, automated responses made to calm anxiety. They can be active or passive. An active response (an interaction of some fashion) seeks control and certainty to calm their anxious concerns. A passive response is one of avoidance, using distance or delay to remove the anxious circumstance. There are several elements in meetings that seem to be the cause of anxiety, and as such, we can use them to organize our assessment. These elements include: Difference, Decisions, Emotion, Responsibility, Trust, and Openness (see appendix A for a quick assessment guide)

Difference

Difference refers to anytime variance or contention comes to the surface in a meeting. This could be differences of perspectives, values, or priorities. The reactive person will often manage the anxiety caused by apparent differences using a few strategies. First, they may use humor to eliminate different opinions. Humor is a difficult thing. When used constructively, it can cut tension and invite others to relax and be at home in the process. However, it can also be used to subtly reject an idea as stupid and thus unacceptable. Humor does not display open conflict and can remove a threatening idea. Another strategy is to discredit the source of an idea. If the person delivering the idea is not credible, then we won't have to seriously consider their point of view. This is a common source of sabotage, a subject we explore further in chapter 5. A third common strategy is that ideas can only come from the same few people. This is a passive action to deal with anxiety. People who question their place do not raise opinions that challenge the status quo or differ from the dominant assumptions represented in the conversation. This is in contrast to groups where ideas come from a variety of people and more importantly a variety of perspectives. This collaborative action invites others deeper into the conversation as full contributors. One last collaborative action that stands opposed to the reactive responses we have discussed is to explore different ideas to create new understanding. In fact, this is what collaboration is about—considering ideas that come from very different perspectives and creating a new understanding as a result.

> Gathering ideas from a variety of perspectives invites others deeper into the conversation as full contributors.

Decisions

Brainstorming and exploring options for decisions are the easy parts. It is when a decision must be made that anxiety grows. Decisions have consequences and some people are more risk-averse than others. There are two kinds of reactive responses generally seen when decisions are being made. On one hand, there is the quick agreement. The first idea to land that has any logic at all is adopted right away. This is reactive because there is rarely any real exploration of alternatives. It is simply an idea that is quickly accepted to make the issue go away. Often these kinds of decisions do not have much staying power. Their life is generally over when people leave the room. A second reactive response is to avoid making a decision at all. The group will talk and talk around the issue but no resolution or decision is made. At these times, groups may go off topic "chasing rabbits," as the phrase goes. To contrast this, the collaborative response is to fully explore alternative views and come to a decision that has commitment. Rather

> The collaborative response is to fully explore alternative views and then commit to a decision.

than forcing something quick out of a need to be comfortable, this kind of decision will last because it is a result of many people learning from each other and coming to a new understanding.

Emotion

Although we recognize that anxiety is an emotion, here we are talking about the presence of any emotion in a meeting. For many people, the presence of any emotion—anger, frustration, sadness, embarrassment—creates an increased level of anxiety. Partly because at some level we know that when emotion is present something important is happening. A second reason is that emotion is viewed as unpredictable and can bring a level of messiness to a meeting. So, for the anxious person who is simply reacting toward the emotion in the room, one of the most common responses is to just avoid the emotion. People sit awkwardly waiting for the emotion to dissipate. Eyes turn downward, people fidget in their chairs, and they may try to change the subject or even comfort a person—not to connect deeper but to get the emotion to leave. This is a time when humor can once again be used to change the tenor of the meeting. Another possible reaction goes in the opposite direction—people over-react. At the first sign of emotional activity, people can just let go of all their pent up emotion. When this happens, the reaction seems to be out of proportion to the event. People tend to present arguments that are full of assumptions, most of which are exaggerated to the extreme. Finally, people may simply take control or attempt to in the chaotic situation. Some people get really loud, some people try to use their authority to demand a certain kind of behavior, and some may simply adjourn the meeting. When group members have a collaborative mindset, their response to emotion is quite different. First, there will be an awareness and even an acknowledgement of the emotion in the room but people will be able to stay focused. They will continue to dive into the subject and maybe even discuss the source of the emotion in order to really understand the perspectives in the

> Emotion is viewed as unpredictable and can bring a level of messiness to a meeting.

room. There will be a tolerance for the discomfort that may be present and patience for those who need to work through their emotional response. All of this leads people to be flexible. By this, I mean they do not let their fear drive them to a place of certainty but rather continue to listen deeply and seek new and shared understanding. Emotions are a terrific sign that something important is happening.

Responsibility

Many times when decisions are being made or problems are being solved, group members will have to press through things that are not working. How they deal with personal responsibility in this situation reveals a good deal about the level of maturity and self-definition present. Reactive responses include blaming others or circumstances for the current condition. They may also look for a leader to fix things. Self-interest will be a higher priority as they seek to justify, absolve, or move responsibility away to other people. Alternatively, mature, self-defined members recognize and take responsibility for their part in the current condition. They have the ability to step back emotionally from their actions and see them more clearly. This also comes with members focusing on their sphere of influence. They may acknowledge other contributing factors but, in the end, they realize they can only control themselves and that is where they stay focused. Also noticeable in this type of setting, members are as concerned with shared success as they are with personal

> Collaborative leaders are as concerned with shared success as they are with personal success.

success. This is different than being a door mat and laying down personal values and perspectives for the group. That is just a different type of reactive behavior. The mature person will seek solutions that allow the group to be successful while not violating their own values and perspectives.

Trust

Trust is often difficult to gage but there are markers that will let you know if there is real trust in the room or if there is just an absence of conflict. Of course, if the trust situation is really bad, there will be open conflict or tension. The reactive response to the requirements of trust will be to not ask for help, to not share information, and often to try to micro-manage others. By the way, micro-management is always about the fear of the micro-manager rather than the limitation of the one being managed. In contrast, collaborative and mature group members will ask for help when it is needed, they will offer information without a need to control how it is used, and their focus is to empower others and build on the contributions of others.

> "Is there real trust in the room or just an absence of conflict?"

Openness

Finally, the level of openness a person presents will give you some idea of where they are. Reactive people need to be right, they do not accept the input of others but rather have a reason or excuse as to why the input will not work. When we need to be right, we also do not learn from our experience. Rather, we will justify, rationalize, or just avoid reflecting on experience. Self-defined responses are the opposite. The self-defined person will seek to understand others, particularly people who disagree with them. They will seek input from others, realizing that alternative perspectives reveal new insights. These are people whose motive is to purposefully learn from their experience.

> The self-defined leader seeks input from others, realizing alternative perspectives reveal new insights.

Alternative Ways of Building Other-Awareness

We do not always have the luxury or the perceived freedom to use real-world meetings to grow our awareness. In fact, in the beginning, it may be difficult to listen to the process of an interaction and be fully present to the content. So, we may need other places to practice that are less consequential if our dual awareness fades. Some of the best tools I have found are movies. Movies show the dynamics of human interaction, often in an exaggerated form. This makes it easier to learn to see what is often subtle in real-world interactions. Movies also allow us to rewind, to see an interaction many times as we consider and make sense of what we are seeing. Though not necessary, a guide can be used (see appendix B) to map interactions. This takes a movie and turns it into a still shot that can be looked at in its entirety. Some great movies to start with are *12 Angry Men* (Fonda & Rose, 1957), which is an entire movie about decision making and one person's attempt to challenge the assumptions of others. *Hoosiers* (De Haven & Pizzo, 1986) is a great movie to look at the impact of change and leadership in a system that is emotionally charged and where people are too close emotionally. The television show *Everybody Loves Raymond* (Rosenthal, 1996-2005) is an excellent study in how emotion and anxiety work themselves out in a family context. It is especially good at revealing how dynamics set in childhood can follow a person into adulthood. Once you begin to pay attention to how people influence others, how they respond to anxiety, and how they do or do not take responsibility for their actions, you will find that you can see it in many places.

Conclusion

The goal here is for the self-defined leader to be able to recognize and understand what is happening in complex human interactions. It is developing the ability to listen to process (how people are acting) and the content (what they are talking about) at the same time. Our aim is to be able to listen to ourselves and to others in such a way that we can assess the dynamics present and do things intentionally to change and improve the interactions. Being self-defined and promoting collaboration is never a finished work. Each time it requires a high level of awareness and intention. When we stop doing the work, our natural tendencies to react and seek comfort, certainty, and control will reappear. It is just too deeply wired into who we are.

CHAPTER FIVE

Developing the System: How to Help Others Become Self-Defined

"Action-learning requires engagement and commitment and comes with consequences. It helps us mature and become more effective in how we work and live."

The real power of self-defined leadership is in its ability to help others develop their own level of maturity. Self-defined leaders who participate from this orientation promote maturity, responsibility, and collaborative action naturally. In fact, it is possible to be intentional about helping people move to a place of full participation if we can establish the proper container.

A container is a combination of values and principles, work practices, and ongoing feedback that creates tangible, intentional opportunities to practice collaborative leadership. The kind of change or maturation we are talking about is the process of making that which is deep-seated and automated, conscious and intentional. It is change at the identity level. This will take a particular environment that is not often noticed nor practiced in organizational life. Self-definition is like any other practice. We must put in the work and intention to move it forward or we will fall back into reactive patterns.

Building the Container

Changing at the identity level is unique. Information and technique are not enough to create the kind of change necessary to become self-defined. Here we want to suggest that three things can help reform the identity of individuals to the point where real collaboration is possible. First, there is **Practice**. Take advantage of any opportunity to accomplish the work in an effective and collaborative way. By its very nature, this reshapes how we work with others, how we think about things, and our natural response to various situations, particularly those where anxiety is present. A second element is **Presence**. Presence refers to the demeanor and actions of important people in our environment. These may be people of status and position or not. What is important about them is that we consciously or unconsciously see them as models who represent something we want to be. For the purposes of collaboration, these people present a non-anxious presence in the room (i.e., they demonstrate calmness in the face of stress, clear thinking in the presence of strong emotion, and stand for what they think regardless of how others may react to it). Finally, there is **Perception**. Perception refers to what we believe to be true and important based on the stories we hear or the stories we see. As we discussed earlier, these are images of what we believe to be the good life. Often, because of the nature of images and stories, we are not conscious of what we are learning. The learning happens more at the emotional level than the intellectual. This does not mean that stories cannot be a means of reforming our values and desires. We just need to become more intentional and aware of their impact. In this chapter, we talk about each of these elements, starting with Practice.

The Practice of Action-Learning

So we come back to where we started. One of the best containers for practice is meetings. That is, meetings that are done with the purpose of collaboration in mind. The best process I have found to develop collaboration and self-defined leaders at the same time is built on a set of principles that align uniquely to promoting collaborative interaction and personal responsibility. This process is simple enough to be useful in a wide variety of settings. When done well, participants encounter all the necessary challenges to deepen their personal and team awareness. The process is called action-learning.

The beginnings of action-learning go back to England in the early 20th century to Reg Revans, a young man studying at Cambridge University. He was in contact with a group of Nobel Lauriat's who met on a regular basis to discuss issues and learn together. In fact, Revans conceived of action-learning as "Comrades in adversity, learning from and with each other through discriminating questioning, fresh experience and reflective insight" (Revans, 1945, as cited in Smith, P.A.C., 1997, p. 721). This small group of men talked differently than most people, and in their spirit of inquiry, Revans began to conceive of the process he would come to call action-learning.

As a process, action-learning involves someone, the presenter, who brings to a small group of committed colleagues an issue that is not easily solved. The group, through careful, probing questions, helps the presenter isolate the real issue to be solved and generates options for the presenter to consider. The presenter honors the input of the group by committing to take action on the issue. At a later time, the presenter comes back to the group to describe what happened and reflect on the action taken. In this way, group members get to learn through the experiences of others. This is a process that can be the backbone of collaborative problem-solving. It can be the framework

> The process of action learning can be the backbone of collaborative problem-solving.

for a peer mentoring process for people who are trying to improve or learn something new. It is useful in decision-making as people work their way through clouded issues. It is the most common process I teach to organizations trying to shift their culture and deepen their level of collaboration.

The real strength of action-learning is the mindset that it seeks to develop through three key foundational ideas. The first principle is **Respect Boundaries.** Most people are reluctant to ask for help. Although there are many reasons for this, one that stands out to me is people are afraid others will take over and resolve their issues for them. This strips them of responsibility, freedom to choose, and eventually the dignity to manage their own life. Action-learning is rooted in the idea that good problem-solving requires people to manage and respect boundaries. This means group members are there to assist the presenter; however, it is not their job to solve the problem. The person who has responsibility for the action to address the issue is the presenter.

> The group members are there to assist the presenter; however, it is not their job to solve the problem.

Consequently, the action that is chosen does not have to be approved by the group. There is no need for consensus. The presenter is the one who will experience the pain if the issue is not resolved and it is the presenter who guides the conversation toward those things that will be most helpful to address his or her issue. Often in the flow of the conversation, the presented issue will morph into multiple issues. It is the presenter (owner of the issue) who, with the assistance of the facilitator, helps the group discern which of the emerging issues or themes is most important, and therefore the one to pursue. When this principle is violated, the group or a member of the group will take too much ownership of the issue and begin to try to move the presenter toward a particular answer or action. We are now back to emotional awareness. The crossing of boundaries is typically due to the anxiety of others who want a quick resolution. To fully get to the root cause can be a messy process with much ambiguity. This, for some, is quite a taxing state. Yet, allowing others to own their issues is a key step in maturity. The most helpful thing we can do in this process is to allow the presenter to work at his or her own pace.

> To fully get to the root cause of an issue can be a messy, ambiguous process.

This does not mean that members cannot challenge the presenter's thinking or surface assumptions or point out incongruities in logic or thought process. However, at the end of the day, the solution is the responsibility of the presenter.

A second foundational principle is **Share Your Ignorance**. Revans noticed the group of scholars did not get together to talk about what they knew nor did they work to demonstrate their intellectual superiority. Rather they engaged each other with humility and were willing to share their ignorance. Sharing our ignorance encourages each person in the process to enter the conversation with a clear willingness to let go of his or her certainty and listen intently to others. The presenter is open to letting the group reframe or at times even change the definition of the issue brought forward. This is because the presenter does not have certainty about the issue. The group offers input in the spirit of gift. There is no certainty on that side of the conversation either. As a result, feelings are not hurt if questions or advice or perspectives are not accepted or helpful. The real goal is just to keep the conversation going, trusting that an answer will become clear if all are willing to hear each other.

This is the single most transformative idea of the process. Most meetings go awry because people come with minds made up and spend their time trying to bring people around to their perspective. They come to the table with certainty of their position and a commitment not to be changed. Sharing our ignorance opens our minds and calms our fears about being wrong. Being right or wrong is not the point. Being helpful is the goal.

> Most meetings go awry because people come with minds made up and spend their time trying to bring others around to their perspective.

> Being right or wrong is not the point. Being helpful is the goal.

The final grounding principle is **Maximize Difference**. In most conversations that attempt to be collaborative, the need for consensus seeks to drive out difference and bring all members into agreement around the "right answer." The strength of the action-learning process is to pull as many different perspectives into the conversation as possible. This shows up in the broad

> The strength of action-learning is to get as many different perspectives into the conversation as possible.

range of questions that are asked and in the variety of solution options generated by the group. The leader of the process (the facilitator) listens carefully for perspectives not represented and often inserts a unique perspective to the conversation. The key here is to voice the unrepresented perspective but don't get married to it. Once it is heard and the group members progress in the conversation, the facilitator/ leader can step back and allow them to find their own way again.

There is one more idea, which is not a foundational principle but is necessary for this work. There must be a high level of trust for people to talk openly. This means there must be a high level of confidentiality. If I am a manager and I am using this process for my area, it is okay to ask if people are participating but it is up to the presenter to decide what and how much to share with whom.

> There must be a high level of trust/confidentiality for people to talk openly.

What Do We Talk About in Action-Learning?

In essence, action-learning is a place where we get help from our peers so anything could be discussed. However, there are some issues that provide more depth and help us more than others. Remember, we are not only solving problems in this process, we are reshaping how we go about solving problems. **The first criteria is that we want to talk about problems and not puzzles.** A puzzle is something that has a clear answer; you just don't know what it is. For instance, how to program the voice mail on your cell phone. You can talk about it all day but, in the end, there is just one way to do it. Find a manual or someone who has the same phone and learn the steps. This is helpful but not likely to reveal much about ourselves nor change the way we think through issues. So, we are looking to talk about problems. Problems are issues with no known solution or with multiple possible solutions that are unclear. I will make one caveat. This same process can be used to explore successes as well. Often we succeed but are not sure why or how to repeat the success. It is just that problems generally bring more energy to the process because when we fail to solve them we feel discomfort until we do.

The issue we discuss should be real and challenging. When we come to this process, we are not interested in talking about hypothetical situations. First, one cannot really take action in a hypothetical situation. Second, hypotheticals do not raise the level of intensity and urgency that real issues do. Remember, people are giving valuable time, energy, and effort to help the presenter. We should be sure they are working toward something that really matters.

The issue should have real value for the organization. This anchors the scope of issues in areas that the group is likely to be able to help. It is not that personal issues are not discussed; however, the context of the discussion should focus on those things that are interfering with or limiting our effectiveness in our roles in the organizations.

The issue should also be within our sphere of influence. The goal of this process is to equip the presenter to take action. We cannot take action on things that are outside our control or beyond our influence. Again this helps to protect the scope of what we talk about and keeps us from turning the process into just a place to complain and blame. I am often asked if we can talk about other people. My answer is yes, as long as you realize the group should end up helping you, the presenter, decide what to do about the situation. Sphere of influence keeps us focused on our personal responsibility in the situation or issue rather than on trying to change others. For example, when a person is in conflict with another person, a good portion of the issue presentation is about what

> Recognizing our sphere of influence keeps us focused on our personal responsibility in the situation rather than on trying to change others.

the other person is doing and the hardship on the presenter. What is often missing is a discussion of the roll of the presenter in the matter. In action-learning, the team and facilitator will help point the conversation back to what the presenter can do about the situation rather than what the presenter wishes the other person would do. This is not to shift blame to the presenter but rather help the presenter find the power they have in the relationship, which is to change themselves rather than trying to change another.

Finally, **the issue should be something that requires us to take action.** Dealing in theory does not have the same effect on us as actually doing something. Action requires engagement and commitment and comes with consequences. It helps us mature and become more effective in how we work and live. Now, sometimes the action we take is nothing. We recognize that our best strategy is to wait or to gather more information before taking action. The difference is, we

Table 5.1: Topics Discussed in Action-Learning

Category	Distribution	Examples
Professional Role Development *Issues concerned with gaining competency in one's roles.*	35% of issues raised	The most frequent issues were around work and time management: • Not willing to ask for help or say no • How to process a performance review • How to be a more assertive project manager
Organizational Membership *Issues concerning one's participation in the organization.*	24% of issues raised	The most frequent issues concerned project assignments and role choices: • Not having enough work • Needing a mentor and feeling isolated
Customer Relationships	17% of issues raised	The most frequent issues concerned managing customer expectations: • How not to strong-arm a client • How to deal with unrealistic customer expectations
Personal Development *Issues addressing personal health and well-being.*	13% of issued raised	• How to balance the urgent and the long-term • How to improve verbal communication
Career Development *Issues around career choices.*	9% of issues raised	• How to continue education • How to handle potential downsizing
Co-Worker Relationships *Issues concerning the interaction between two or more co-workers.*	2% of issued raised	• How to set boundaries • How to effectively confront another

are doing this on purpose and with good reason rather than just to avoid a difficult or uncomfortable situation.

Knowing what to talk about is often the biggest initial hurdle for teams starting action-learning. It is often difficult to identify good topics. I did a study on the topics discussed in action-learning that might be helpful here. We had an organization that imbedded action-learning as a peer mentoring process and faithfully used it over the course of three years. This topic review included 50 different sessions reflecting 89 different themes. We looked at facilitator notes from sessions and identified core themes around which we could organize the topics. Table 5.1 shows the kinds of things that were discussed and sample issues presented.

The Flow of Action-Learning Dialogue

Action learning is a process that disciplines us in how we think through issues. There is an ebb and flow to the conversation. Adhering to the flow will keep us true to the process and keep us from devolving the conversation into a venting session. The important characteristic of this flow is that it moves from specific to broad to specific to broad to specific. In a sense, there are two movements to the conversation. One is about discovery and definition while the second is about solutions. Each movement also comes with some pitfalls that tend to distract us from our task and take us astray. Figure 5.1 provides a picture of the flow of action learning.

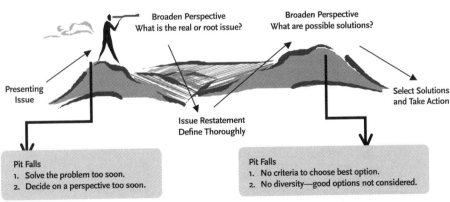

Figure 5.1 Dialogue Flow Diagram: The Path of Inquiry, © 2007, Robinson, *Teams for a New Generation*

The process starts with the presenter describing their issue. This is a **specific** idea or better yet a specific question. The group then should broaden the conversation, using questions. We do not want to assume that the issue presented in the real issue. Often, we are most aware of the symptoms of an issue, and that is what we present. The group asks questions to help us understand the real and root cause of our issue. This takes some courage and patience because the group may change our understanding of our issue. This is good. Solutions to the wrong problem will not resolve our issue. Another pitfalls into which people step is trying to solve the issue as soon as it's presented. This is the wrong move, because to move that quickly we are making an enormous number of assumptions—unchecked assumptions of which we are probably not aware. So questions protect all involved from making assumptions which might not be true. A second pitfall, related to the first, is accepting one perspective too soon. When we are in discomfort, we want understanding and clarity. We are tempted to accept the first perspective that seems to make any sense of our situation; however, that perspective might be wrong or at least incomplete. We need to stay true to the process and go **broad** by asking questions from a variety of perspectives even if they seem afield from the issue.

> Often, we are most aware of the symptoms of an issue, and that is what we present.

After we have broadened the conversation with a thorough questioning, we get more **specific** for a moment as the presenter decides on the real cause of his or her issue. It is here that some discernment is needed. It is usual that in exploring an issue, we find there are two or three possible causes or multiple issues wrapped in the presenting issue. So the presenter, who owns the issue, needs to decide on which one to focus. He or she decides on which ideas to ask for the group's help.

The process then goes **broad** again as the group brainstorms possible solutions. The goal at this stage, like the first, is to get as many perspectives and options on the table as possible. It is important for group members to remember they are offering options, not trying to get the presenter to make a particular choice. It is not the group that will feel the pain if the action does not work. It is not the group's issue. So in the spirit of sharing our ignorance we offer our insights and advice tentatively, allowing the presenter to use what is helpful and discard the rest. We do not get our feelings hurt or take it personally if our ideas are not accepted. Being the one with the right answer is not our goal.

> Group members must remember they are offering options rather than trying to get the presenter to make a particular choice.

> We do not get our feelings hurt if our ideas are not chosen. Being the one with the right answer is not our goal.

Now there are a couple of pitfalls in this movement of the conversation that can also stall progress. First, when ideas start flowing, the presenter can have a difficult time deciding which is best. This can be a time when well-meaning team members overstep and start making choices for the presenter. The presenter does not need to be rescued by someone else making the choice; he or she does need a set of criteria to evaluate options. This is how group members can help. One, they can articulate that a criteria set is needed and second, they can help brainstorm what that criteria might be. The second pitfall occurs when there is no diversity in options. Often a good idea surfaces and the group moves quickly into the details of a single idea. Diversity is missing. So the group needs to be disciplined to get a variety of ideas on the table before diving into the details.

In the end, the conversation gets **specific** once again as the presenter chooses which action or actions to take. Remember, this is not a consensus exercise. The group does not have to approve of the presenter's chosen action. At this point, the only responsibility of the group is to ask about outcomes at a later date. This provides a little accountability but mostly a chance to learn from the presenter's experience.

As groups work through a presenter's issue, they may discover it is a shared issue, meaning many members of the team have a part in the issue. They may also realize that many members of the group share the same issue but in different contexts. It is perfectly fine to expand the ownership to all who share the issue. Just remember that in the end, each person chooses his or her own actions in response to the issue. These actions do not have to be the same for all. Each will have to go out, take the action, and learn from his or her own experience.

Practice is important because it forms us. By that I mean it shapes our way of thinking, responding, and acting. So how does action-learning form us? I can say with some assurance there are a several ways. Many times, I have heard people who have used action-learning say it changed the way they interacted with others and it changed the way they participated in all their meetings. First I would say that action-learning invites us to enter our inquiries with humility. As Covey (1989) wrote many years ago, seek first to understand and then be understood. The very form of action-learning requires us to ask, question, and seek before we determine a way forward. Second, it helps us understand that the best way to be helpful is to come alongside rather than take control. Collaboration would be easier in organizations if people could trust that when they ask for help, they will gain partners rather than have their issues taken away.

> Action-learning invites us to enter our inquiries with humility, to come alongside rather than take control.

Purposeful Experience

In the early 1990s, organizations in large scale were using experiential-based training as a means to develop leaders, build teams, and promote values in their workforce. For many, this took the form of challenge course programs. The more adventurous partnered with organizations like Outward Bound and used outdoor pursuits like backpacking, rock climbing, and white-water rafting as their classroom. Though today, the enthusiasm for this method has waned, there are still practices out there that are using purposeful challenge and experiential methods to develop people. Whether an organization uses the outdoors or indoor problem-solving scenarios or simulations, the use of experience to teach ties it all together. All of these methods include a similar formula: a problem that must be solved by taking action followed by intentional reflection to understand what happened and what was learned.

In the debriefing of such experiences there is plenty of good information, awareness, and new understanding to be shared. However, if we use the lens of formative experience to view these practices, we might find that there is something more important that comes from the dialog than the insights in the moment. As we have said, self-defined leaders are people who have a high level of awareness of their own thoughts, feelings, and values as displayed in their actions. What if this cycle of action and reflection develops this deeper level of awareness more than we think? I want to suggest, that this experiential practice can help people develop in the following ways.

First, experiential learning creates a reflective mindset, which promotes curiosity rather than certainty. Self-defined leaders continually try to make meaning and gain clarity about not only what they do but why they do it. Not only are they interested in their

> Experiential learning creates a reflective mindset, which promotes curiosity rather than certainty.

own motivations, they are also trying to gain that sense of clarity about others and promote the same kind of self-awareness with the people around them. This requires a real sense of curiosity. The willingness to ask questions in order to gain better understanding, regardless of the answer that might be found, is at the heart of self-definition and it is the driving force of collaboration as well. Yet, in order to be curious, we must be willing to give up our need for certainty. Certainty is an illusion that promises us security and safety. If we know for sure some particular truth or right idea, then we can relax and feel secure. The fact is, we generally only know in part. It is the ongoing ability to add to our knowledge

> In order to be curious, we must be willing to give up our need for certainty.

and wisdom that keeps us not only current in our understanding but flexible to respond to the next generation of challenges. In his article, Martin (2005) writes that about 50% of the problems leaders have to solve today cannot be solved with knowledge from solving past problems. There is a real need for adaptability in our world today. We must realize that adaptability is more than gaining new information. It requires a level of courage and curiosity that must be developed over time. It must be formed in us because when we are scared and uncertain, we will never think our way into clarity. If we are not curious at our core, we will always seek security and certainty first.

Secondly, experiential learning teaches us the value of confession and affirmation. This is a strange thought I know, but I believe one of the most limiting factors to our ability to lead well and work collaboratively is shame. At the heart of shame is the fear that we will be driven out of our community because we did something wrong (Brown, 2012). So to counter this fear, we generally hide those things that do not work, the mistakes we make, or the actions we take but only partially understand. At the heart of experiential learning is meaning-making (i.e., the ability to make sense of an experience and learn from it). This learning includes what went right but also what went wrong.

> Experiential learning teaches us the value of confession and affirmation.

The underlying tension in the questions of reflection are what worked and how do we do more of that in contrast to what did not work and how do we do better next time. Again, this happens on an intellectual level, but it is our adaptive unconscious (Smith, 2009; Wilson, 2002) that shapes what we are willing to see. It tells us what is a threat and thus needs to be avoided. We need to develop our willingness to experience discomfort in the service of something more important. Action and reflection teach us that it is okay to confess mistakes or actions that do not work out in order to find a better way. It helps us trust that when we are honest, talk with respect, and listen deeply to others, we will find a better way. We also realize that it is okay to take credit for what we do that is right. In fact, it is only when we affirm the ways we work or the actions we take that we are able to repeat success intentionally.

> Meaning-making is at the heart of experiential learning.

So we have described Practice, the rituals if you will, that can be embedded into organizational life to form in us the necessary attitudes to grow in our maturity and work collaboratively. But practice is only one part of the development container.

Perception

It is amazing how stories and experiences stick with us. If I were to ask you to describe your life, most likely you would tell me stories. You would not outline a set of propositions that guide your life. You would tell stories. We tell them because that is how our minds work. We need to realize the stories we tell—who we promote, or who we seek input from—all shape the way people around us see us and the workplace as a whole.

Every organization has stories to be told. Insights given to new employees. Images that show up in signs and posters. Unspoken approval given through secret meetings and good offices. What we choose to talk about shapes the culture and assumed beliefs of the people we work around. I worked for a company once where it seemed that coming up with that new idea—seen as a "home run"—was the driving force. If you came up with such an idea, then you would be selected by senior leaders to jump multiple steps in terms of title and influence. Now, I never saw this happen but it was a real driver none the less. How did this come to be? Maybe because there were subtle ways that people who stayed late were presented as more committed. Possibly it was because secrets (i.e., information that was not out for public knowledge) were shared mostly after hours or in the late nights of retreats. No one was ever told this was the way it was but it became a reality which drove wedges between coworkers. Members became protective of their information, their models, and their clients; they spent more time protecting their turf than working toward solutions that would benefit the company.

> Every organization has stories to be told. What we choose to talk about shapes the culture and assumed beliefs.

The most powerful stories are those of leaders who take a risk and act contrary to the dominant assumptions. For instance, one of my clients had a CIO who was attempting to move the department in a new direction. When the vision was articulated, there was immediate resistance and upheaval. He

> The most powerful stories are those of leaders who take a risk and act contrary to the dominant assumptions.

quickly backed down and his initiative never did happen. In contrast, within this same information technology organization, a director and his manager attempted to completely change the model for how technology services were delivered. They started with a group of people left over from a downsizing. No one really wanted to work with that group. Yet at every turn, these leaders did the bold and courageous move rather than retreat. The typical thought in an experiment would be for leaders to take more control; however, these leaders gave more freedom. When it would seem prudent to position yourself in opposition to peers that are resistant to change and would inhibit your work, these leaders made this group their board of directors. When talent was hard to come by, it would seem prudent to hang onto the best and brightest, yet these leaders let their best project manager walk because he would not get on board with vision.

These are the images, the stories, that founded a new organization that was successful in the face of opposition from high in their own department, for over a decade. We teach every day. The question is are we teaching on purpose.

Presence

In chapter 3, we looked at a definition of presence as a leadership strategy. As a reminder, **presence is the ability for people to remain calm in the face of anxiety and by their demeanor empower courage and openness when things are chaotic.** Here we want to look more deeply at how presence impacts the dynamics of the system. If a person is to help dissipate anxiety and promote collaboration, then there are two aspects of the human system that must be understood. These are the forces in tension within the system and the role of sabotage to promote the status quo.

Forces in Tension

Inside every system there are two forces always in tension with each other. These forces are paradoxical in that though they are opposite and conflictual with each other, both are required for the system to be healthy over time. On one hand there is the force of **individuation** which is the drive to stand for oneself. It is the desire to make one's own way in the world, to think for oneself, and to take responsibility for one's future. It is why we grow up and go out into the world to make our own way. On the other hand, there is the force of **togetherness**. Togetherness is what motivates us to belong. It is why we join clubs, communities, churches, and such. It is what brings us together with others. Brown (2012) says that we are hard-wired for connection. This is the force of togetherness.

> We are hard-wired for connection.

I want to bring together the works of a few people to help us understand the details of this struggle and how it undercuts a group's ability to work well. In Figure 5.2, a polarity map (Johnson, 1992) outlines the specifics of the dynamics. Language from the work of Adam Kahane (2010) helps us gain a better understanding.

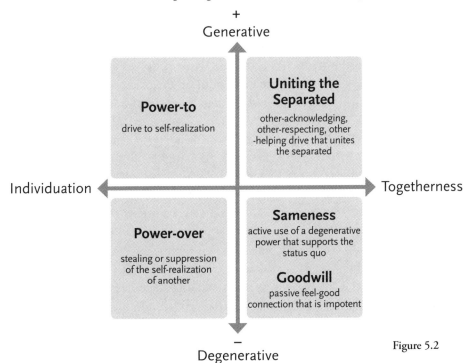

Figure 5.2

As we said, there are two forces in tension that create what Johnson would call a polarity. It is a paradox of sorts. Though the forces are opposite, both are necessary over time for health and effectiveness. Additionally, each force has an up or positive quality, called "generative" as well as a down or negative quality called "degenerative." We tend to get the degenerative effects of one force when we are focusing on it to the exclusion of the other.

The generative side of **individuation** has to do with responsibility and, as Kahane (2010) puts it, "power-to." It is the ability to make a contribution and realize one's unique presence in the community. It is the power to take action in life and to do so out of one's own particular abilities.

> Generative individuation is the ability to make a contribution and realize one's unique presence in the community.

When however, we focus exclusively on individuation, we get the down side of it which Kahane describes as "power-over." It is when we are trying to achieve our own actualization by suppressing or stealing the power of others. For instance, if you were trying to make a name for yourself by taking credit for the work of another, you would be entering into power-over. This happens most often when people of power use their power to get their way at the expense of others.

When we realize the best of **togetherness**, we are, as Kahane (2010) says, bringing together what is separated. This involves a state of trust and collaboration in which individual contributions are freely given to the group in service to a higher purpose. The down side of togetherness is triggered when anxiety is high. Togetherness is the natural response to fear as we tend to be stronger together than alone. I have seen both a passive and active form of the dark side of togetherness. The passive way is that of goodwill. Goodwill is often mistaken for trust when it is really just the absence of open conflict. It is not trust because it has not been tested. Trust must face conflict, difference, and disagreement and survive. Goodwill is only a fragile pseudo peace. Many group problems are

> Goodwill is often mistaken for trust when it is really just the absence of open conflict.

a result of members not being willing to risk rocking the boat and testing their relationships to see if it is trust or only goodwill.

> Trust must face conflict, difference, and disagreement and survive.

The down side of togetherness is sameness. Sameness is the need/desire to make all members of the group the same. They need to think, feel, look, and act the same. It may start as a seduction, bringing in those who are outside. We can tell whether or not it is healthy by asking how it responds to individuation. Sameness does not leave room for original thought or tough questions. It is held in place by absolute loyalty to the dominant way of the group. It can be seen in the peer pressure of adolescents or in the certainty of particular religious communities. If the group cannot convert the person, it will surely seek to eliminate that person.

A particularly alluring process to sameness can happen. It is one with an appearance of trust but is in the end uniquely devastating. Like many things, what allows sameness to take hold is an level of trust. Yet, this trust is an illusion that is permeated by secrets, hoarded information, and gossip. For those in the know, there is a feeling of privilege and worth that continues to seduce people into this state of sameness. Once in, people may not challenge the status quo because of the allure of the power or special status they feel. Others stay engaged out of fear. Though they may not fully agree with what is going on, they have seen what happens when one tries to go one's own way. The backlash and venom that comes from suggesting there is something not healthy about this state of sameness is often quick and fierce. It can be overwhelming.

This leads to a particularly devastating dynamic. When groups are anxious, it is often a result of not only the dysfunction in the overall organization but also the anxiety in the lives of individual members. When the anxiety level is high enough and there are those who stand in the way of achieving togetherness, the group will often identify a scapegoat on which to focus the anxiety

> A group's anxiety often stems from both the dysfunction in the overall organization and it's individual members.

of the group (Girard, 2001). The scapegoat is blamed for the ills of the group and is often demonized in order to be driven out or at least discredited. The scapegoat tends to be the weakest, newest, youngest, or least liked in the group. The anxiety of the whole is transferred to the one individual so the group will feel better. We see this in groups where one or two members are labeled "not team players" and are removed one way or the other from the group. Interestingly, with that person gone, someone else eventually moves into the same role. The group, which is unable or unwilling to face its own anxiety, will always need a common enemy or scapegoat to mask their own fearful state.

So how do we manage this tension with our presence? The solution is twofold. First, we need to reinforce the value of the upside of the polarity with which we are struggling. For instance, if the group is being consumed by goodwill or forces of sameness, we recommit to being a healthy and collaborative group. We also look to the opposite upper side of the polarity map (page 69) for guidance. We overcome sameness and restore balance by returning to a focus of personal responsibility and contribution. This involves becoming aware of our impact on what is happening. If we are a part of the system, we contribute to how it is behaving. So we start by asking ourselves this question, "What am I doing to increase anxiety or not doing that allows anxiety to go unchecked?" The second question to ask ourselves is, "What, within my sphere of influence, can I do about the current behavior of my group?" I often ask team members that question in this way, "What could you do now other than what you normally do to create a different outcome?" In this way, we do not get caught waiting for someone else to make things different. We step out in courage to lead, to influence, not necessarily because we have a formal responsibility but because we have awareness of what is and a vision for what could be.

At the heart of this is simply having the courage to challenge the assumptions that are distracting or controlling the group. We can do this by naming what we see going on, in a calm not coercive

> We overcome sameness by returning to a focus of personal responsibility and contribution.

or blaming way. We can ask questions that help bring to the surface the assumptions being held and thus reveal the dynamics of the group. This can come from the formal leader, but it can

> It takes courage to challenge the assumptions that are distracting or controlling the group.

also come from anyone in the group who becomes aware of what is going on. If we are the formal leader, we have an extra level of responsibility to respond to these dynamics in a non-anxious manner. We can also serve the group by taking the steps through our presence and practice to reduce or remove as much anxiety as we can from the group. Clear communication, clear purpose, transparent decision-making, connection, and a free flow of information all help reduce the anxiety of the group even if they experience elevated stress outside of the organization. We can help create a more peaceful container, which enables better interaction.

Sabotage

Sabotage is an automatic response of the system to someone who is promoting change in that system (Friedman, 1999). The goal of sabotage is to get the person who is acting in a self-defined way to go back to the way they usually are so the system can go back to being the same. Now, we need to realize that often this response is automatic and mindless. People sabotaging the leader are not typically consciously aware of what they are doing or the desired effect they want to have on the system. It is simply a way of being that has helped those persons deal with anxiety in the past. It is important to know that, as we attempt to change the way things normally are in a system, there will be reactive responses. If change— moving from protective to collaborative action—is to be sustained, the leaders of

> As we attempt to change the way things normally are in a system, there will be reactive responses.

the group must see sabotage for what it is and respond to it in a way that holds onto the vision of a better way. "Another way of putting this is that a leader can never assume success because he or she has brought about a change. It is only after having first brought change and then subsequently refrained from changing back in order to calm down the resulting reactivity that the leader can feel truly successful" (Friedman, p. 304).

Sabotage comes in two forms. One is to undercut the leader (Friedman, 1999) by raising doubts about his or her competence. It makes you question the certainty of your actions. It makes you wonder if you have overstepped and are going in a direction that could be problematic. It feels like blame. It often sounds like accusations. In sophisticated forms, it appears to be condescending. The key is to remember it is not about you. It is about the anxiety of the system in response to the change. Undercutting can also take the form of discrediting a person. It can include a questioning of your qualifications, motives, and character. It can take the shape of a person making a loud and emotional case for the risk of what the leader is trying to do. Often this includes a number of exaggerated assumptions meant to raise the level of anxiety in order to get others in the system on board.

> The key is to remember sabotage is not about you. It is about the anxiety of the system in response to change.

The second form of sabotage comes as seduction (Friedman, 1999). Seduction plays out in the goodwill, friendship, or familiarity of a person to bring the self-defined leader back into place. This person may offer "helpful" advice because you're friends. Seduction banks on the leader's fear of rocking the boat and disrupting what seems to be a good thing. There is an illusion of trust but the trust is not real because it is not able to withstand challenge.

An enjoyable and excellent way to teach yourself to see the dynamics of sabotage can be found in movies. One of the best movies for learning the patterns of seduction is *Hoosiers* (De Haven & Pizzo, 1986). In one of the opening scenes, the new coach, played by Gene Hackman, goes to the local barber shop to meet the town folks. One of the indicators of something amiss is when people seem to take a strong interest in something that should not be that important. In this case, most of the townsmen gather to "welcome" the new high school basketball coach. Both undercutting and seduction are present in this scene. Seduction comes in the form of the interim coach offering to help him until he gets settled. Another member steps forward with a big smile and a firm handshake while he tries to confirm the coach's preference of defenses. Even the local minister gets on board with his confident assumptions presented as a test. After some pleasantries, which do not get much information out of the coach and thus calm the uncertainties of this unknown quantity, one member just goes right at it. He questions why the superintendent hired someone who has been in the Navy for ten years, thus hoping to put the coach on his heels. He then tells the coach what is required for him to succeed; he must get the town's best player, Jimmy Chitwood, playing again.

Now all of these moves are meant to make the coach respond in a way that will make the town feel comfortable. On a side note, often groups that are anxious cannot see their way clear to choose leaders who might help them out of their current situation. The question is, How does a self-defined leader respond to a situation like this? In this scene, the leader simply listens for a while and then politely excuses himself without ever commenting on their desires, veiled threats, or being drawn into the debate about types of defense. In this situation, he has no way to really win or promote any change among this group. Changing this group of people is beyond the scope of responsibility of his role and there is no amount of discussion or data that is going to change their minds. Anxious people who are overly involved in the affairs of others will only change when they either come to the awareness that they need to change and manage personal boundaries better or when they are made to respect boundaries.

If we are in a situation where we have no real authority to set boundaries, we must simply be sure we do not get pulled into the debate. If we are pulled in and get emotionally invested in one outcome or one side of the argument, we have lost our ability to help. The best we could do is name what we see going on (see the film guide in the appendices for *Hoosiers–Walk to the Door* scene). Sometimes if the group is near a state of changing, this can help them pause and see what they are not paying attention to in the moment. If however, we have some position of authority or permission of the group to

Sabotage will always present as one or more people trying to influence a person into being a certain way.

intervene, promoting the respect of boundaries is key. By this, I mean that we should own what is ours to own and let others be responsible for their choices and actions. Sabotage will always present as one or more people trying to influence a person into being a certain way.

Now this might seem a bit indirect and it is. Remember we cannot force others to change. If we try, we will just sustain the anxiety in the group. We must do the right thing because it is the right thing. In doing so, we encourage those who are mature enough to risk change and collaboration with us. It is the star player in the movie who comes back, based on what he sees in the coach's presence that is the key.

I will say one more thing, if we want to help a group change, we will, even as positional leaders, need allies. These are mature members who are open to trying new things and capable of taking responsibility for themselves. These are the people that are typically held down by the immature members of the group. Mature allies pursue solutions that have mutual benefit to all affected parties. They will do what is best in the long run rather than what is most expedient in the moment.

The key for dealing with sabotage is to first remember, whatever the "issue" of the moment is, that it is not the real issue. It is only the thing that starts the rise of anxiety. Second, to be a helpful influence, regulate your own responses without being overwhelmed or held captive by the reactions of others. Do not be consumed by the need to change those who do not want to change. Rather look for those who are willing to take a risk, think differently than the status quo, and show signs of personal responsibility. These are the potential allies that can help move things forward.

We cannot force others to change. We must do the right thing because it is the right thing. In doing so, we can encourage others to risk change and collaboration with us.

CHAPTER SIX

Triangles and the False Hope of Gossip

"If we truly want to be collaborative, we need to understand the
nature of conflict and how we can deal with it in a way that is
energizing and empowering rather than destructive."

The group walked to the middle of the room. Half of the
participants lined up single file looking at the other half also lined up
single file. As instructed, participants reached down and picked up
the rope on their side of the line. What do you think happened next?
Yep, this group of adult professionals immediately started their own
tug-o-war.

I have found over the years that tug-o-war is a great image to
teach people about conflict. Tension, disagreement, and conflict will
eventually be present in every group. It is a natural outcome of diversity
and, in fact, a key component for trust and
sustainable solutions. Conflict is not the
problem. The problem is that we do not
understand conflict, and we certainly do not
know what to do with it. At one extreme, we

**Conflict is not the problem.
The problem is that we do
not understand conflict.**

avoid it and thus insure that real trust will not be present in a group.
Or we attempt to win at any cost and thus insure that real trust will
not be present in a group. If we truly want to be collaborative, we need
to understand the nature of conflict and how we can deal with it in a
way that is energizing and empowering rather than destructive.

Conflict Strategies

Let's go back to our tug-o-war. How can we win a tug-o-war? The strategies that are used in this event are the same strategies that many people use in order to win in conflict.

Linear Strategies

An often-used strategy, if one is gifted with size, power, a strong voice, and an intimidating stare, is **brute force**. Many people learn over time that if they get big enough, loud enough, and forceful enough, people will cave in. Often the sheer force of personality is enough to convince people to go along, regardless of the quality of the idea. Other people learn to just dig in and hold on. **Perseverance** will lead you to victory. In many a meeting, the person who talks the longest often emerges as the winner. A third strategy is to use **deception** to throw people off balance. In a tug-o-war, once the other team is pulling hard on the rope, let about 2 feet of rope go all at once. While the other team is off balance reacquire the rope and pull for all you're worth. While the other team is down, your team can walk off with victory. In conversation, this deception can look like exaggerated assumptions, holding information until the last minute, or using logic to pin someone in a corner. A final strategy is **avoidance**. Some people do not enjoy a good tug-o-war and when they discover that is the meaning of the rope, they simply let go and refuse to participate. In the end, the conflict is resolved because it is never acknowledged. However, it will resurface another day.

Triangles

The strategies we've looked at so far are pretty straightforward. We learned them as kids and have developed our favorites. It is a linear view of conflict where one side is right (generally my side), one side is wrong (typically the other side), and the goal is to make the other submit. To be honest, this is an easier form of conflict with which to deal. It tends to be pragmatic and since the strategies are automated, a good dose of awareness can just wake us up to better strategies.

There are, however, more subtle and dangerous ways of dealing with conflict. These are strategies that operate in the system as a whole. They are difficult to see, easy to deny, and not only do they not resolve conflict, they move anxiety around the system so that everyone but the owner of the issue will struggle. These take the form of a triangle. If we add more ropes to our tug-o-war setup, we will be able to model this in real time for our groups.

The basics of a triangle, which some (Kerr & Bowen, 1988) say is the foundational structure of relationships, involves three people and some conflict (see figure 6.1). For our purposes here, a triangle forms when there are two people who are in conflict with one another (the darkest arrow indicates conflict). There are a couple of different ways that those in conflict can minimize the anxiety and tension arising from their conflict in this scenario. First, persons B can approach person A as a confidant, attempting to gain A as an ally. This could result in A getting involved in the conflict in order to resolve it for B. A might do so by convincing C s/he is wrong and to go along with B. A's attempts to influence C may be subtle or may be a power move. It can also be a slow ostracizing of C, with A and B ganging up on C and using a gossip campaign to eliminate C's influence in the group. In families this happens quite often. Say couple (B and C) are fighting. One or both turn to a friend, parent, or sibling (A) to plead their case. If A becomes an ally, A will feel responsibility to intervene, which in the end results with A feeling the stress and anxiety of the conflict. This is true because A cannot fix a conflict between B and C.

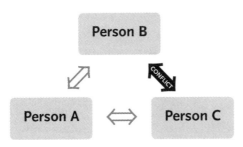

Figure 6.1 Conflict Triangle

Only B and C can fix it. This triangle can be applied to co-workers and leaders, or between departments or teams. It can be scaled to any system level.

A second scenario would involve B and C ganging up on A as a common enemy. In this case, the strain between B and C lessens as they focus their energy on a common foe. Since the perceived threat from A is greater than the conflict between B and C, they make A the primary source of their anxiety. This works as long as there is a common enemy. When A goes away, the conflict between B and C returns. So for peace to endure, B and C will always need a common enemy. This often happens in team conflict. Members of a team get frustrated with each other. Often, a well-meaning leader may focus their attention on someone (a competitor or other problematic person or team) outside of the team. Magically, the tension between the team members goes away. However, it is only a short-lived truce because the underlying issue between team members has not gone away.

A Systems Approach to Conflict

To eliminate unhealthy conflict in our teams, we cannot keep looking at it from a linear perspective. In that frame of mind, there is always someone who is right and someone who is wrong. The focus remains on the other person who is not like us. In a systems mindset, the focus is not on the other as an enemy, it is on the relationship that is not working. In conflict, there is a relationship that is not providing what it is supposed to. It is not working and each member of the conflict is contributing something to making the relationship not work. In systems theory, this is called mutual influence.

> In a systems mindset, the focus is not on the other as enemy, it is on the relationship that is not working. In systems theory, this is called mutual influence.

When we stop trying to change the other person and focus on understanding what we are doing to contribute to the conflict, we can find resolution. When we understand our part, we have something upon which we can act. The question is, "What can **I** do to make this situation better?" We cannot force change on the other, but we can change ourselves and thus influence the other person. The two parties can actually join forces on something they have in common, the relationship. The reason triangles are so dangerous to teams is that they keep our attention focused on others. We do not consider the fact that we are contributing to the conflict and so our self-awareness remains low. We then feel forced into various strategies to coerce, discredit, and defeat the other.

> Triangles are so dangerous to teams because they keep attention focused on others.

Triangles can be healthy only when the third party is used to help us gain perspective, vent emotions, and clarify our part in the process. In the end, the answer to the following question tells us which way we are moving, "Are my actions promoting personal responsibility and mutual understanding of the conflict?" If not, the only way we can help a conflict between B and C is to make sure B and C are talking to each other. Any other scenario only perpetuates the fight.

Tolerance of Tension

There is one more thing that is important for us to realize if conflict is going to be resolved and potentially useful. The presence of tension can push us into automatic responses to conflict (triangles, defensiveness, and avoidance). Not all tension is bad. Often, tension arising from differences can be quite creative. Tension is the result of people holding different perspectives. It becomes a problem when everyone involved needs to be right. However, if we do not panic in our tension, we can

> Tension is the result of people holding different perspectives. It becomes a problem when everyone involved needs to be right.

see things we could not see alone and new and often more sustainable solutions emerge to our issues. In the end, as we have discussed, the self-defined leader will grow their awareness of and tolerance for discomfort. Rather than panic, they choose to listen intently and understand what each perspective offers to the situation.

Illusions of Trust

Before we end, I want to offer a word of warning. Triangles are seductive because they often lead to secrecy, inside information, and perceptions of specialness for being brought inside the conflict as a confidant. We must see this for what it is. Secrets and gossip promise a security in relationships based on information that others do not know. It provides an illusion of trust. It is not real trust because real trust cannot be based on deception, withholding of information, or actions that threaten exclusion. When we succumb to the false promise that we will be given some special place of value if we join in the secret talk, we end up with the anxiety of the other person. It is not trust because that line of action is expedient to relieve the stress and anxiety of the other person. As soon as the secret alliance no longer does that, it is of no use to the other person. It is also not uncommon for the person who brought us in to betray us, using information shared in the secret, inside talks with others when it is expedient to do so.

> Secrets and gossip provide an illusion of trust.

Trust only comes from honesty, transparency, and authenticity. Trust involves informed choice and is only stable when mature (self-defined) persons chose to be vulnerable and open. Anything born out of an immediate need to relieve discomfort will not survive in the long run.

> Trust only comes from honesty, transparency, and authenticity.

Conclusion

I want to wrap up this exploration of collaborative culture with a reminder that collaboration, like power, is a thing of paradox. We fail to work together because we are afraid. Afraid to lose control, afraid to be vulnerable—we seek certainty. But when we give influence away, it not only allows others to understand our perspective, it allows their perspective to change ours. We create more, not less.

Many tend to believe that power is a zero sum game—there is a limited supply of power and so when others gain some, we lose ours. This upside down view of the world does not comprehend the deepest truths. When we give away power, when we allow others to contribute, we generate the space for more influence, i.e., more power. Collaboration is the same. The more we give away in terms of ideas, curiosity, influence, and trust, the more possibility is created.

> The more we give away in terms of ideas, curiosity, influence, and trust, the more possibility is created.

We need mature people who know what they think and why they think it but who come together humbly, knowing that even in their current clarity, they may only know in part. We need questions driven by earnest curiosity that will demonstrate respect and consideration for ideas that are very different from the norm. We need the courage to step up and speak truth when it is not popular and to wait for the better solution though all around us are clamoring for instant relief. These are things that anyone, in any role, in any organization or team can do.

I'll close with a story that illustrates my point. A few years ago, I was leading a team in a ropes course experience. The group and especially the leader had little interest in anything related to learning or improvement. They wanted a day out of the office. Needless to say, the motivation of the group was low and my expectations limited. There was a lady, the administrative assistant for the group, who was not there to take it for granted. She was in her late fifties or early sixties. Unlike the faculty and dean, who regularly participated in professional development, this was a treat for her. Now, I did not inquire about how she felt, but given her comments and my own experience of working in a college setting without a doctorate, I sensed she felt inferior in this group. Even so, she did not let their lack of enthusiasm nor my concern for her physical ability limit her. At the end of the day, when we were debriefing the lessons learned, I really only heard one voice, hers. No one else was willing to speak up because no one else had put anything into the day. Yet to this day, I remember her statement to this group: "The thing I learned today was that every voice counts." She was not willing to let circumstances nor those around her determine her effort, her openness, and her willingness to take risks and learn.

This is the image I want us to take away. Collaboration is possible when every member of a group, organization, family, or team is willing to do what he or she can. We may not all have the knowledge, insight, or authority, but we all can have curiosity, respect, and the willingness to listen intently. To do so, we must have an understanding of what makes us anxious and how those things impact our choices, actions, and views of others. We can establish practices that not only encourage our talking and listening but also shape the unnoticed beliefs and values that determine what we see and focus on in the first place. When we foster new minds that can see what is hidden to us currently, we will be able to change our world in a way that lasts.

> We may not all have the knowledge, insight, or authority, but we all can have curiosity, respect and the willingness to listen intently.

Acknowledgements

The section on Action Learning has developed for me over the last twenty years. I want to acknowledge the great variety of authors who have helped me understand the idea. Too many years have passed to parse out where each idea initiated so I wanted to mention the works that shaped my thinking on the subject here for your ongoing investigation.

- Bunning, R. L. (1997) A manufacturing organization action learning programme that has paid bottom-line profits, *Career Development International, 2(6),* 267–273.
- Keys, L. (1994) Action learning: executive development choice for the 1990s, *Journal of Management Development, 13(8),* 50–56.
- Marsick, V. J., Cederholm, L., Turner, E. & Person, T. (1992) Action-reflection learning, *Training and Development, August,* 63–66.
- Mumford, A. (1995) Learning in action, *Industrial and Commercial Training, 27(8),* 36–40.
- Parkes, D. (1998) Action learning: business applications in North America, *Journal of Workplace Learning, 10(3),* 165–168.
- Revans, R. (1945) *Plans for recruitment, training and education in the mining industry* (London, Mining Association of Great Britain).
- Revans, R.W. (1991) Action learning—its origins and practice, in: M. Pedler (Ed.) *Action learning in practice (2E)* (New York, Gower).
- Smith, P. A. C. (1997) Qing action learning: more on minding p's and q's, *Management Decision, 35(5),* 365–372.
- Smith, P. A. & Peters, J. (1998) Action learning and the leadership development challenge, *Journal of Workplace Learning, 10(6/7),* 284–291.
- Weinstein, K. (1997) Action learning: an afterthought, *Journal of Workplace Learning, 9(3),* 92–93.

Meeting Review – Quick Assessment Guide

Reactive Responses		**Collaborative Responses**
☐ Uses humor to eliminate different opinions ☐ Discredits different ideas ☐ Ideas come from the same people	**Difference**	☐ Explores different ideas in order to understand ☐ Ideas come from many different people
☐ Decisions are avoided ☐ Quick agreement	**Decisions**	☐ Commitments reached after thorough discussion
☐ Emotion is avoided ☐ Overreacts ☐ Discomfort when things are uncertain	**Emotion**	☐ Aware of emotion but focus is not lost ☐ Flexible
☐ Blames others or circumstances ☐ Looks for someone else to change or rescue them ☐ Self-interest more important than shared success	**Responsibility**	☐ Takes responsibility for the problem, decision, or mistake ☐ Focuses on what can be changed about themselves ☐ Shared success more important than self-interest
☐ Does not ask for help ☐ Does not share information ☐ Micro-manages others	**Trust**	☐ Asks for help when needed ☐ Freely shares information without trying to control how it is used ☐ Empowers others
☐ Needs to be right, defensive ☐ Does not accept input from others ☐ Does not learn from their experience	**Openness**	☐ Seeks to understand those who disagree with them ☐ Seeks input from others ☐ Intentionally learns from experience

Appendix B

Movie Guide: Hoosiers

Scene: heavy hand

One of the dynamics in groups is that there is a great desire for things to remain the same. Those who have benefited from the status quo will become anxious at any signs of something that will trigger change. Consequently, there are often actions of sabotage towards the leader who might introduce real change. One type of sabotage is seduction. Seductive sabotage looks on the outside to be passive or even friendly on the surface, but the goal is to get the leader to play a role that will allow the status quo to continue.

Reflection Questions

- What types of seductive sabotage do you see in this scene?
- How does the leader (Gene Hackman's character) respond?
- Why do you think this is a good response to sabotage?
- How would you have responded?
- What types of seductive sabotage do you see in your life (from coworkers, family, friends)?

Comments

Seductive sabotage shows up in the big smiles and firm handshakes as the new coach enters the barber shop. It can be seen in the not so subtle introduction of the preacher. It is also seen in the statement of the old coach that they will give the new coach a hand until he gets settled in. It is an effort to both feel out where the new coach is at and hopefully "bring him into the fold" through the power of acceptance.

You also see the undercutting sabotage. The man who questions why a sailor who has not coached in over a decade is hired to coach their team. The new coach is quietly coerced through statements like zone defense is the only one that will work for us. There is a calling into question the credibility of the new coach. All efforts to get the new coach to toe the line in this new community for him.

Response of the Leader

The leader in this scene simply listens for a while and then politely excuses himself without ever commenting on their desires, veiled threats, nor does he get drawn into the debate about types of defense. In this situation, he has no way to really win or promote any changes among this group. Changing this group of people is beyond the scope of responsibility of his role and there is no amount of discussion or data that is going to change their minds. Anxious people who are overly involved in the affairs of others will only change when they either come to the awareness that they need to change and manage personal boundaries better or when they are made to respect boundaries. Later in the movie, Jimmy Chitwood, the town's star player, makes such disturbance to the town. In a meeting designed to continue this starting meeting to the final conclusion (to remove the coach that would not be controlled) he says he will play but only if the coach stays. Since they care most about living through the basketball team, this action allows some space for change as this force of informal authority enforces a boundary for the coach.

Scene: Walk to the Door - this scene immediately follows the Welcome to Town scene and involves the coach and a female teacher. Scene 4 on DVD Scene Selections Menu

Key Concept: Responding to the Reactivity of Others

Anxious systems, where members are emotionally immature or invested in the actions of others in an unhealthy way, will have high levels of reactivity. Reactivity is an automated emotional response that comes out of the fear of the one reacting. It amplifies anxiety and can lead to very dysfunctional behavior that limits the effectiveness of a team or organization. One way to think about reactivity is that it is "an overreaction" to a benign action, statement or question.

Reflection Questions
• What signs of reactivity do you see in this scene?
• How does the leader respond?

- What do you think is appropriate about his response?
- How would you have responded? Why?

Comments

The female teacher is the reactive one in this scene. She first becomes very defensive about an innocent comment about the small town. Later she is not convinced that the coach will leave Jimmy alone and continues to berate him. She shows typical signs of reactive behavior. She is defensive, overly emotional and overly serious about the situation.

The leader (Gene Hackman) does several good things in response to this reactivity. The mature leader will not be drawn into an argument started by another person's reactivity. He stays calm, but does not cut off the relationship. Rather, he continues to engage her and in fact goes deeper than her statements and simply states out loud the essence of the conflict. She does not respond so he does not push, but he has just created transparency about the real underlying issues. If she would have engaged him on that level, their relationship would deepen. Otherwise, she will just change the subject because the real issue is out in the open. Secondly, he remains playful with situation. He tries to joke and takes a final light-hearted response to her fears about him meddling with Jimmy. This less serious response does two things. First, it keeps him from getting to upset of anxious himself. It also extends the opportunity for the relationship to improve and deepen without trying to force something on the other person. Remember the leaders response to a reactive person is less focused on changing that person and should be focused on remaining calm himself/herself as well as dissipating the anxiety in the group or situation.

References

Argyris, C. & Schon, D. (1974). *Theory in practice: Increasing professional effectiveness.* San Francisco: Jossey-Bass.

Baumeister, R. Vohs, K., DeWall, C., & Zhang, L. (May, 2007). How emotion shapes behavior: Feedback, anticipation, and reflection, rather than direct causation. *Personality and Social Psychology Review v11 n2*:167.

Bohm, D. (1996). *On dialogue.* London: Routledge.

Bowen, M. (1966). The use of family theory in clinical practice. *Comprehensive Psychiatry, 7*: 345-374.

Bowen, M. (1976). Theory in the practice of psychotherapy. In Guerin, P. J., *Family Therapy.* New York: Gardner Press.

Bowen, M. (1978). *Family therapy in clinical practice.* Jason Aronson, Inc. New York & London, .

Brookfield, S. (1987). *Developing critical thinkers.* San Francisco: Jossey-Bass.

Brown, B. (2012). *Daring greatly.* New York: Gotham Books.

Cherniss, C. & Goleman, D. (2001). Training for emotional intelligence: A model, in Cherniss C. & Goleman, D. (eds), *The Emotionally Intelligent Workplace*, p. 209-233, San Francisco: Jossey-Bass

Covey, S. (1989). *The 7 habits of highly effective people.* New York: Fireside.

Cranton, P. (1994). *Understanding and promoting transformative learning.* San Francisco: Jossey-Bass.

Cross, R., Martin, R., & Weiss, L. (2006). Mapping the value of employee collaboration. *The McKinsey Quarterly 2006 Number 3.*

Deloitte. (2016). Report: Human Capital Trends.

Dickinson, W., deGruy, F., Dickinson, L., Mullins, H., Acker, S., & Gilmer, V. (1996). The family systems assessment tool. *Families, Systems & Health, 14(1),* 57–71.

Ellinor, L. & Gerard, G. (1998). *Dialogue: Rediscover the transforming power of conversation.* New York: John Wiley & Sons, Inc.

Ernst, C. & Chrobot-Mason, D. (2011). *Boundary spanning leadership.* New York: McGraw Hill Education.

Friedman, E. (1985). *Generation to generation: Family process in church and synagogue.* New York: The Guliford Press.

Friedman, E. (1999). *A failure of nerve: Leadership in the age of the quick fix.* Bethesda, MD: The Edwin Friedman Estate/Trust.

Frost, R. (1916). *Mountain interval.* Henry Holt And Company.

Ghoshal, Sumantra, & Bartlett, C. (Jan, 1996). Rebuilding behavioral context a blueprint for corporate renewal. *Sloan Management Review, Vol. 37,* pp 23 (14).

Girard, R. (2001). *I saw Satan fall like lightening* (Williams, James, translator). Maryknoll, NY: Orbis Books.

Goleman, D. (1998). *Working with emotional intelligence.* New York: Bantam Books.

Hansen, M. (2009). *Collaboration: How leaders avoid the traps, create unity and reap big results.* Boston: Harvard Business Press.

Heron, J. (1992). *Feeling and personhood: Psychology in another key.* Thousand Oaks, CA: Sage Publications.

Isaacs, W. (1999). *Dialogue and the art of thinking together.* New York: Currency.

Johnson, B. (1992). *Polarity management.* Amherst, MA: HRD Press, Inc.

Johnson, P., Buboltz, Jr., W., & Seemann, E. (Spring, 2003). Ego identity status: A step in the differentiation process. *Journal of Counseling & Development, No. 81,* pp. 191-195.

Kahane, A. (2010). *Power and love: A theory and practice of social change.* San Francisco: Barrett-Koehler Publishers, Inc.

Kegan, R. & Laskow Lahey, L. (2009). *Immunity to change.* Boston: Harvard Business School Publishing Corporation.

Kegan, R. & Lahey, L. (2016). *An everyone culture: Becoming a deliberately developmental organization.* Boston: Harvard Business Review Press.

Kerr, M., & Bowen, M. (1988). *Family evaluation.* New York: W.W. Norton & Company.

Kloppenborg, T. & Petrick, J. (Summer, 1999). Meeting management and group character development. *Journal of Managerial Issues, Vol. 11, No. 2,* pp. 166-179.

Kunnanatt, J. (2008). Emotional intelligence theory and description: A competency model for interpersonal effectiveness. *Career Development International, Vol. 13, No. 7,* pp. 614-629.

Lowney, C. (2003). *Heroic leadership.* Chicago: Loyola Press.

Martin, A. et al. (2005). *The changing nature of leadership.* Center for Creative Leadership Research Report.

Maslow, A. (1943). A theory of human motivation. *Psychological Review, 50,* 370-396.

Mezirow, J. (1991). *Transformative dimensions of adult learning.* San Francisco: Jossey-Bass.

Mezirow, J. (Spring 1998). On critical reflection. *Adult Education Quarterly, Vol. 48,* p. 185, 14 p.

Mishra, P. & Mohapatra, A. (Jul-Sep 2009). Emotional intelligence in the occupational setting: A literature-based analysis of the concept and its measurement. *South Asian Journal of Management; 16,* 3; ProQuest p. 86

Murdock, N., & Gore, Jr., P. (September 2004). Stress, coping and differentiation of self: A test of Bowen theory. *Contemporary Family Therapy 26*(3).

Olson, E., & Eoyang, G. (2001). *Facilitating organizational change: Lessons from complexity science.* San Francisco: Jossey-Bass.

Quinn, D. (1999). *Beyond civilization.* New York: Harmony Books.

Rawlings, D. (2000). Collaborative leadership teams: Oxymoron or new paradigm? *Consulting Psychology Journal: Research and Practice, Vol. 52, No. 1,* pp. 36-48.

Revans, R. (1945). *Plans for recruitment, training and education in the mining industry.* (London, Mining Association of Great Britain).

Rock, D. (2008). SCARF: A brain-based model for collaborating with and influencing others. *NeuroLeadership Journal, issue 1.*

Robinson, G. (2005). Action learning: Developing critical competencies for knowledge era workers. *Action Learning: Research and Practice, Vol. 2, No. 1,* pp. 79-88.

Robinson, G. & Rose, M. (2004). *A leadership paradox: Influencing others by defining yourself.* Indianaoplis, IN: Author House.

Salovey, P. & Mayer, J. (1990), Emotional intelligence. *Imagination, Cognition and Personality, Vol. 9,* pp. 185-211.

Senge, P. (1990). *The fifth discipline: The art & practice of the learning organization.* New York: Currency.

Skowron, E. (Fall, 2004). Differentiation of self, personal adjustment, problem solving, and ethnic group belonging among persons of color. *Journal of Counseling & Development, No. 82,* pp. 447-456.

Skowron, E., & Dendy, A. (September, 2004). Differentiation of self and attachment in adulthood: Relational correlates of effortful control. *Contemporary Family Therapy 26(3),* pp. 337-357.

Skowron, E., & Friedlander, M. (1998). The differentiation of self inventory: Development and initial validation. *Journal of Counseling Psychology, 45(3),* pp. 235–246.

Skowron, E., Wester, S., & Azen, R. (Winter, 2004). Differentiation of self mediates college stress and adjustment. *Journal of Counseling & Development, No. 82,* pp. 69-78.

Smith, J. (2009). *Desiring the kingdom*. Grand Rapids, MI: Baker Academics.

Smith, P. (1997). Performance learning. *Management Decision, 35(10)*, 721–730.

Stanchfield, J. (2014). *Inspired educator, inspired learner.* Bethany, OK: Wood N Barnes Publishing.

Steimer, T. (2002). The biology of fear and anxiety related behaviors. *Dialogues in Clinical Neuroscience, Vol 4, No. 3*, pp. 231-249.

Steinke, P. (2006). *Congregational leadership in anxious times*. Herdon, VA: The Alban Institute.

Steinke, P. (2010). *A door set open: Grounding change in mission and hope.* Herdon, VA: The Alban Institute.

Steinke, P. (1993). *How your church family works: Understanding congregations as emotional systems.* Herdon, VA: The Alban Institute.

Tang, Y., & Joiner, C. (2006). *Synergic inquiry: A collaborative action methodology.* London: Sage Publications.

Tichy, N. & Cohen, E. (1997). *The leadership engine.* New York: HarperBusiness.

Wilson, T. (2002). *Strangers to ourselves: Discovering the adaptive unconscious.* Cambridge, MA: The Belknap Press of Harvard University Press.

About the Author

Greg Robinson is currently the Associate Professor of Outdoor Leadership Ministries at John Brown University. He is also the Program Director for HoneyRock, the Outdoor Center for Leadership Development of Wheaton College. Greg has also held the role of President of Challenge Quest, LLC in Pryor, Oklahoma, the Managing Member of Adventure Quest Recreation, LLC.

Greg has a Ph.D. in Organizational Behavior and Leadership from The Union Institute and University in Cincinnati, Ohio. He also has a M.S. in Counseling from John Brown University.

Greg's professional career has concentrated in the areas of experiential learning, team development, leadership development, and facilitation and consulting with organizational change efforts. He is the author of *A Leadership Paradox: Influencing Others by Defining Yourself, Teams for a New Generation: A Facilitator's Field Guide, Adventure and the Way of Jesus* and *Lessons of the Way: Using experiential activities to explore the way of Jesus.*